Praise for *The Road to Self-Awareness*

Having known Ian Murphy for over seventeen years, since he first contacted us at the Coming Home Network, I have had the privilege of watching his continued growth in grace and holiness. This, his latest book, is a wonderful, open, and honest sharing of his heart and experience of the growth and maturation that I have witnessed in his life. I praise his courage to be able to openly share his heart and struggles that, by the grace of our Lord Jesus, he has been able to surmount. I strongly recommend this book to anyone who seeks true and lasting healing, whatever the struggle may be.

— *Jim Anderson, Pastoral Care Coordinator,*
The Coming Home Network International

What a wonderful and helpful book. This book is pure Dr. Ian Murphy: his engaging storytelling, good humor, passion for Jesus, vulnerability and honesty, and compassion for all, especially that person (reader) right in front of him.

Sometimes the best way to judge a book is by one's facial expressions. These were mine with this stellar book: smiles from the great telling of a story and well-placed humor, watering of the eyes when compassion arose through my throat to teary eyes, the frown of the brow when I knew I would need to chew on a different perspective or insight, and the deep sigh from a truth that pierced my heart.

Few have demonstrated the dynamism of virtues as clearly as Dr. Ian Murphy's insight into the interconnections of the virtues and how receiving love is the antidote for pride (perfect love casts out fear) and together love and humility creates the strong foundation for healthy self-care.

— *Harvey Payne, Psy.D., Counselor and Psychologist,*
VP Academic Affairs for Digital Learning, Divine Mercy University

With *The Road to Self-Awareness,* Dr. Ian Murphy provides a universal tool applicable to the plethora of therapies available in the world of psychology. Virtue is the glue that first ties and then melts all our moving pieces together into a new beautiful self. This book provides a practical guide to growing in virtue as the expression of love, the elemental ingredient to healing of any kind. Brilliant!

— *Elke Stephan, Cana Family Institute*

Funny, practical, and thoroughly Catholic. This is not another self-help book. You know by now that they don't work. This is a book that teaches us how to accept the help God gives us — and let Him complete the work He's begun in us.

— *Mike Aquilina, Author of* The Fathers of the Church

With important insights and *very* worthwhile!

— *Paul C. Vitz, Ph. D., Senior Scholar/Professor, Institute for the Psychological Sciences, Divine Mercy University*

This book is not only the story of one man's journey of faith, but it is also an invitation to the reader to not only read, but to feel, digest, and enter deeply into this incredible story of healing and conversion. The author invites us to see that this is our story as well, and it challenges us to examine our own life, as we are reminded in these pages that "we are not a problem to be solved, but instead we are the cherished creation of the Living God."

— *Bishop Jacques Fabre-Jeune, Diocese of Charleston*

Jesus once met a man who called himself "Legion," a man who felt shattered and out of control physically, spiritually, mentally, emotionally, and socially. Our Lord put him back together again by healing him holistically—body, mind, and soul. This book can do something like that for you, no matter the affliction.

—*Dr. Tony M. Martin, Professor of Christian Studies (retired), University of Mary Hardin-Baylor*

This book does an amazing job of focusing on the whole of each individual, the inviolable dignity of the human person, and the idea that everyone has the inherent right and ability to heal. This work truly illuminates the idea that we are not a problem to be fixed, but rather a priceless work of art that is worth a high level of care, respect, and restoration.

—*Dr. John West, LPC, NCC, Lead Author of* **Emotional Intelligence for Religious Leaders**

The most enlightening part of this book for me is realizing that I am not a problem to be *fixed*. Rather, I'm created and loved. Dr. Murphy's text offers us practical ways of exploring the implications of this discovery for our daily growth.

—*Dr. Dennis Feltwell, East Campus Provost, Pasco-Hernando State College*

This personal story is a true example of what it means to heal from an integrated approach; seeing one's self through God's eyes and as the author says, finding that "our God is bigger than the daily struggle." It's an understanding of what it means to advance up the "spiral" and to recognize one's worth. A great read!

—*Mallory Wines, Ph.D., LPCC-S, Assistant Professor, School of Counseling, Divine Mercy University*

The Road to Self-Awareness

IAN MURPHY

The Road *to* Self-Awareness

A Therapy Book for Christians

SOPHIA INSTITUTE PRESS
Manchester, New Hampshire

Sophia Institute Press
Box 5284, Manchester, NH 03108
1-800-888-9344
www.SophiaInstitute.com

Sophia Institute Press is a registered trademark of Sophia Institute.

paperback ISBN 978-1-64413-822-9

ebook ISBN 978-1-64413-823-6

Library of Congress Control Number: 2022952217

for Rachel,
who has shared the dream of this book with
me from the first week we met

Contents

PART IV

Healing Breakthroughs from the Heart of the Church

PART V

Abiding in Victory from Here Forward

The Road to Self-Awareness

Introduction

All Aboard

YOU ARE ABOUT to embark on a journey into personal healing that can be profoundly life-transforming—in *any* area of your life where you long to be healed. My own messy tale about the victory God gave me over obesity will help guide you through the universal concepts along the way. Essentially, this is not a book about weight loss. It's a book about healing, with insights that apply across the board. In the end, this is a book about salvation itself—and the ongoing process of our "working it out with fear and trembling" (see Phil. 2:12).

If you could experience real, thorough, and lasting healing in *any* area of your choosing, what would it be? Is it a fractured friendship? A lack of self-control? The tendency to a bad temper that hurts the people you love? Maybe there is some trauma that haunts you, or an addiction, compulsive tendency, or dysfunction that—no matter how hard you try—you can't seem to get under wraps. Are there insecurities, misspent energies, or toxic relationships that rob you of your fullest happiness? Or perhaps, like me, disrupted routines, overcrowded schedules, and undisciplined struggles with self-care have propelled you into overeating to an extent that is harmful to your health. No matter the area for which you seek this authentic

3

and permanent healing, the strategies we're about to explore will apply to you; they will help you to achieve it.

Using Parable and Explanation

When Jesus taught, He utilized both stories (such as the Parable of the Good Samaritan, which demonstrates mercy in action) and instructional explanations (such as the Sermon on the Mount, which explains the virtue of mercy). I attempt to imitate this inimitable style throughout the book by moving back and forth between my ongoing personal testimony and corresponding relevant theological investigations. To this end, each chapter begins with a specific aspect of the ongoing narrative of my weight-loss journey and then moves into a discussion about universal healing concepts that correspond with that particular episode from my life.

Inevitably, these two sections of each chapter will overlap here and there because the two are inseparably connected. We see this in the particular stories and universal truths taught by Christ. Nonetheless, the general movement from ongoing narrative to explanatory discussions provides a useful structure, one which benefits from the strengths unique to both story and explanation alike.

The Imagery of a Spiral

Regarding its style, this book is composed in the manner of an upward spiral. I first encountered this literary form in reading Pope St. John Paul II's encyclicals. When I began to read his work, I confess that, in my ignorance, I felt as though I were trying to sort through a stream of consciousness in order to find his point. I found myself saying, "This is repetitive. How could such a brilliant man be so redundant, yet not realize it? He already said this on several occasions, and I got it the first time. This keeps going in circles." Yet, as

I humbled myself and really let it in, as I *received* from him, I came to realize how wrong I'd been.

He was not venting a stream of consciousness, being redundant, or speaking in circles. On the contrary, I am convinced that he knew exactly what he was doing, with a distinction that marks the world's finest artists. He was, in a sense, writing in the same way that people grow. Envision, if you will, a winding pathway that starts at the base of a tall mountain and encircles it until reaching its zenith. As you journey along the uphill climb, there certainly is a circularity to it. Yet, it's not a circle—it's a *spiral*. A circle is endless; a spiral is headed somewhere.

A spiral offers us a three-dimensional symbol that, while perhaps seemingly circular, adds the vertical dimension of either declining or advancing across time.[1] Any growing person who is ascending maturity's path will recurrently stumble in the same areas, for we all continually struggle against our particular weaknesses and disorders on this side of Heaven. Yet if we are truly growing amidst our stumbling and fumbling, as Christ's disciples grew, then we're not on an endless circle. Advancing up the spiral, even though we keep circling back to the same areas, we hit them at a higher elevation each time. We can then say, "I've been here before, yet I see more now. Viewing my life from a higher vantage, I am better at recognizing this pattern. I see what leads up to this point, and where it goes from here."

Since a spiral illustrates growth—or, as sometimes happens, decline—it gives us an ideal framework for discussing the ascendant path of salvation. Whenever John Paul II repeated some earlier theme from his writing, he was revisiting it from a higher vantage point, casting richer meaning upon the topic with each encounter. With a prayer for humility, I do my best to mimic his effective format in this book.

You will, therefore, encounter a number of recurring themes, including the image of God, the blinding nature of vice, the importance of humility, the baby steps of habit formation, body-soul unity, the role of our emotions, and the power of the Holy Spirit. Each successive review is purposeful. By returning to these recurring and united themes at higher elevations, we shall reach heights and insights that are unattainable in any simple, linear sequence.

Real Healing Cannot Be Rushed

Unfortunately, we live in a postmodern society of quick-fixes, sound-bites, immediate gratification, instant texts, microwaved food, and precooked answers to internet searches from across the information superhighway. Our fast-paced "McCulture" has trained us to expect direct, speedy responses and solutions to all of our inquiries and problems. If we take a moment for honest introspection, we will likely realize that we've succumbed to this pace—and the expectation of it—in our own lives. How many times have we thought, "Let's get to the point already" or "Yeah, *got it*—can we move on now, please?" I've even heard people flaunt their speedreading abilities with boasts such as, "I can read almost a thousand words per minute with 85% comprehension!" That would be like saying, "I can shovel down my dinner five times faster than the average person, while still tasting 85% of my food!" This "reader" just admitted that 15% of the meaningful content he was perusing was sacrificed—in other words, not read. With that analogy in mind, remember this caveat: this spiraling voyage into healing isn't something to speed-read. By its nature, this is not a book to be skimmed. *Salvation is not a soundbite.*

Call to mind all the most significant elements of your life. For me, they include my friendship with Jesus, my marriage to Rachel, and my Ph.D. in Theology. Do you know what all of these blessings have in common? None of them was achieved quickly or easily. Rather, each one was the fruit of painstakingly slow growth and solid commitment. Maybe you are a consecrated celibate, a medical professional, or a public servant. Or perhaps you are a parent, a missionary, a lifelong friend, or any combination of such honorable callings. Whatever the case, can you recall the training, practice, courage, and sheer sacrifice you endured to get to where you are in your profession, friendships, or vocation today? Childrearing, for one certain example, is no insta-click, nor are any of life's most meaningful relationships and roles. Healing is likewise.

Not a Self-Help Book

Regarding its content, the publishing world could categorize this work as a self-help book—which is funny, because my journey revealed that I was utterly *unable to save myself.* "Self-help" is an ironic designation to be sure, as the Catholic worldview flips many commonly perceived secular notions on their heads. We'll revisit this idea later; for now, I simply wish to express that this volume is not your usual companion to personal healing. It's not your typical therapeutic book. On my road to victory, I encountered my capacity to fall on my face repeatedly, the limits of my willpower, and my weakness for all things peanut butter. More importantly, I realized my complete dependency upon grace. I saw my radical need for God, for my friends, and for their love.

No doubt, I tapped into unprecedented power—the power to reduce my bodyweight by 33% and keep it off! However, this was not accomplished through the empowerment of rugged individualism nor the self-made champion. I did not stand mightily against my foe upon my own strength, saying, "The demon of gluttony shall look upon me and quake, for I am Lion-Man, Slayer of Body Fat." I was not taking the reins of my own life, being true to myself, and plowing through all who would stand in my way. On the contrary, I discovered my need to die to myself in order to find life. It was a journey of vulnerability, brokenness, repentance, and receptivity to a transcendent power beyond myself—Christ's power to deliver, heal, and transform. As I allowed the Lord to saturate my inmost spirit more deeply than ever before, the power I encountered was one in which God alone is glorified, while I am the grateful beneficiary of a gift.

An Important Disclaimer

Since my illustrative narrative regards weight loss, I want to say up front that I am not a dietitian, nor am I a therapist. I'm a Gospel missionary, one who has experienced deliverance firsthand and seeks to pass along that which I've learned. If weight loss happens to be a specific area in which you seek personal healing, of course I hope my story can be an instrumental aid for you. However, I do want to be clear that this book is no replacement for professional nutritional counsel, spiritual direction, or medical advisement from your doctor.

What This Healing Expedition Is Not

On a somewhat related note, this exploration into healing is not a dietary guide to the biochemical mechanics of losing weight; again, it applies broadly to a variety of needs, of which gluttony is just one example. The fact of the matter is, when I was trying to lose weight, the surface details about diet and exercise were ultimately not enough. These material mechanics by themselves led me down one dead end after another; I would lose some weight at first, only to gain it all back. In order for me to be truly delivered with sustainable victory, I needed to integrate those material considerations into a much larger view of myself that included my spirituality. Only then would I be healed—and not just from obesity; the force I had tapped into was a weapon against any vice. Ultimately, beyond defeating vice altogether, the divine power I encountered surpassed merely "getting rid of a negative." It was about the presence of a positive, a doorway into thriving in beatitude and freedom.

I'm not saying that biological factors aren't important. On the contrary, they're an integral part of our body-soul makeup — and I've enjoyed regular appointments with a professional dietary counselor for this very reason. What I'm saying is that biomechanics are not enough by themselves. In their proper place, physical specifics about any problem can certainly be helpful, but numerous skilled professionals in a variety of fields have already published ample material about such things. This book does something different.

What This Healing Expedition *Is*

The present work searches into the unseen foundations beneath issues such as obesity. As my experience testifies, matters surrounding exercise and diet were an outgrowth of deeper spiritual realities. As such, this journey highlights the embarrassingly unsatisfying nature of so-called therapies that only scratch the surface, ignoring the real source of human fulfillment.

Based upon a more comprehensive approach to caregiving, this book is an exploration into who your Creator is, who you are in Him, and how the transforming agency of His grace manifests across your growth. It's about tapping into the power of salvation, curing disorder at its roots, and remembering that "we are more than conquerors" in Christ Jesus (Rom. 8:37). This expedition seeks to demystify the power of grace, to demonstrate how very real and life-changing it truly is, and to get you excited about what our Lord wants to do for you! It is a therapy book, so to speak — one for the growing Christian.

An Invitation

I encourage you, as you embark on this journey, to *trust the process*. One of the chief themes of our exploration into lasting deliverance is that quick-fixes are a lie—they actually keep people trapped in the very disorder that needs healing. I invite you to bracket off any reflexive attitudes trained to expect memes or oversimplified straight lines from A to B. Working out our salvation with fear and trembling is anything but simple. Resist the cultural gravity that favors speed at the expense of substance, and read this book slowly, carefully, reflectively, and prayerfully. Savor every bite. It might seem like bad news that it takes time to afford the topic of healing its rightful treatment, but remember that it also takes time to age the finest wine. The wait is well worth it, and even indicative of its quality. The good news is that, if you trust the process, you are about to encounter healing that is real and permanent.

Whether it's a vice from which you seek deliverance, or the cultivation of a particular virtue you desire, this book will, God willing, provide you with the same life-transforming encounter with the Almighty that set me free. Within these pages exists the opportunity for you to experience that journey and that victory for yourself—which can really only be done when we search for victory in Christ.

PART I

THE QUEST

FOR REAL

HEALING

ONE

The Scale Tells No Lies

The Match-Making Puzzle

I HAD NEVER been on a blind date before, so as I turned the corner to see the girl with whom I'd be spending the evening, I found myself more nervous than anything else. I was typically against the idea of going into a date *blind* for obvious reasons. Risk assessment aside, it simply made more sense to know the person first and have established some level of friendship before trying a date on for size. Yet in this particular case, a trusted graduate-school classmate of mine was playing matchmaker.

Although my friend had no pictures to show me, she assured me, with sincerest confidence, that this mystery girl was "the perfect complement for me in every way." Against my better judgment, I agreed, and we scheduled a meeting at the local baseball park. As soon as I saw her, the most obvious physical attribute that I couldn't help but notice was that this girl was unusually obese.

I never liked the idea of myself as a shallow man with surface-based, one-dimensional standards of romantic attraction. Moreover, when it came to what I was looking for in a woman, the "wife of noble character" from Proverbs 31 described it best. I thus tried to put aside mere physical attributes by themselves in order to give the experience an honest try; but in the end, there was simply no romantic chemistry whatsoever. After leaving our only date together,

I became distraught by the notion that my cupid-playing classmate had described this girl as "the perfect complement for me *in every way.*" It bothered me enough that I decided to confront my friend about it.

"I appreciate what you tried to do, but a *customized fit?*" I questioned.

"I'm so sorry, Ian," my friend replied, shaking her head in embarrassment.

"There's nothing to apologize for," I said, "you didn't do anything wrong. What's bothering me is the idea that you thought she was my perfect complement 'in every way.' When it comes to my physical appearance, does the girl you tried to hook me up with really embody a customized fit for me?"

My friend was speechless for a moment. She had the look of a person caught between two choices: (1) tell the hard truth to somebody who was clearly not ready to hear it or (2) offer some soothing words. I imagined her thinking, "Do I lie? Or is this where Ian's self-image comes to die?"

She eventually replied, "Oh, I totally understand what you're saying, and I'm sorry for sending that message. I just had a one-track mind to set my friend up with such a great-looking guy, and didn't think about anything else."

A glutton for punishment, I attempted another blind date under similar circumstances. I did the same thing as before, expecting a different result—a phenomenon that some suggest as a definition of insanity. Sure enough, in all the ways that mattered, the results were identical, and I even heard the same trite "explanation" that didn't make any sense. It seemed as though my friends were intentionally hiding something from me—either to protect me from something I wasn't ready to face, or because neither wanted to be the one to break the news.

Searching for Answers

Besides, there had to be some rational explanation for why romantic interest in me had ceased of late. Why had such attention recently stopped cold, with my only prospects being the overweight friends of my graduate-school classmates? What were people not telling me? "Maybe it would be easier for a man to tell me than a woman," I thought.

I approached one of my male friends and caught him up on the details of the two failed blind dates as well as the follow-up conversations with each respective matchmaker.

When I asked him for a real explanation, he adopted the same speechless expression as the others. Then a sudden smile came across his face, as though he had just thought of some believable falsehood that would get him out of this jam.

"Do you want to know what it is?" he asked.

"Yes! What is it?"

"Ian, God has put a block on you."

"Huh?"

"A block," he explained. "God has placed a special barrier around you that prevents women from feeling interested in you. Because of how great-looking you truly are, He had to do it. Otherwise, you would have gone down the wrong road. In order to save you for the one girl He has planned for you, God had to block all romantic attraction toward you from anyone else."

Lies seem most effective whenever the liar gets God involved. No doubt, the idea that I was so attractive that the Almighty needed to place a divine barrier around me would have been a comforting thought for me to entertain. Yet flattery has a distinct odor, and my friend's words reeked of it. I knew that he, too, was hiding something from me.

Keeping the Blinders On

Of course, the true issue surpassed the lies of my friends. My real problem regarded the lies I was telling myself. You may be thinking, "If only you had a friend who loved you enough to be real with you when you asked him what was wrong." Actually, I did have such a friend. Gently yet bluntly, he told me that my own *extreme weight gain* was the apparent problem. What fascinates me looking back on this reality bomb was that I didn't feel it go off. My friend couldn't have stated the facts more plainly than he did, but his words didn't register, as though they ricocheted directly off of my head. The reason my classmates had been pairing me up with big women was clear: I was a big man! Yet, I couldn't see it—I wouldn't see it.

Taking the Blinders Off

Eventually and reluctantly, I considered the possibility that I may have put on five to ten extra pounds—maybe. God responded in an unforgettable "wake-up call" experience. As I got ready to give a lecture one day, I noticed that my leather belt was beginning to stretch and tear on the last hole available. I also realized that the elastic waistband on my dress slacks was pulled taut, with no more available give. To my rescue came the very large navy sports coat that covered a multitude of sins. Pulling it snug, I was still able to fasten it with a single golden button on the front of the jacket, which completed the ensemble. I prepared to sit down, feeling satisfied and handsome.

But when I sat down, my giant belly suddenly popped out above my belt to exert pressure against my already-snug sports coat, and then the single gold button shot off the jacket like a projectile missile. The button made a brief whistling sound as it bulleted through the air, followed by a distinct pop when it hit the wall. This soaring button finally woke me from the blinding slumber of gluttony.

I immediately went digging through my storage closets in order to find my old scale. I wiped off the considerable amount of dust that had accumulated on it after years of neglect. It was one of those old circle scales with the dial, on which 360 degrees represented a hundred pounds. For the first time in a long time, I stepped onto it. Quickly, the dial went around the scale's measuring circle once, then twice, then even a third time, as though it was running laps—which was something that, evidently, I ought to have been doing. At only five feet and ten inches tall, I weighed a portly 303 pounds. I hadn't merely gained five to ten pounds; I had put on over a hundred pounds, oblivious to it the whole time.

In a panic, I called my sister.

"Hey, Ian, what's up?" she greeted me.

I asked, "Sarah, am I fat?"

"You didn't know?" she replied.

"No, I didn't. It might sound strange, but I honestly had no idea."

"I figured you knew. After all, you see yourself in the mirror every day," she said.

I responded, "You know, it's the strangest thing, but I didn't see it. I thought I looked like I've always looked."

"I'm sorry, brother. I would have told you if I'd realized you didn't know."

"It wouldn't have done any good. I would have let your words just bounce off like everyone else's."

In my epiphany of self-awareness that day, I knew that I was responsible for my condition. I suffered no thyroid problems, no hormone imbalance, no clinical depression, nor any other diagnosable affliction that can contribute to weight gain. In my case, *poor diet* and *no exercise* were the culprits. I lacked the virtue of self-care, and I was up to my neck in the consequences. I had poisoned myself with the sin of gluttony, a dangerous vice through which I used food as a coping mechanism to escape from anxiety. I shuddered at the realization that the devil had found a way to kill me slowly, and I came to recognize gluttony as a dawdling form of suicide. Whether by cholesterol, liver damage, or an early heart attack, I was eating my way into self-destruction—a deadly sin indeed.

DISCUSSION

The Profound Significance of Ingestion

Gluttony is no mere pesky nuisance, although it enjoys operating unchallenged under this guise. Instead, this fatal sin is a powerful adversary that seeks to disintegrate the very fabric of our existence. I've heard it said that, if you can beat gluttony, then all the other deadly sins will fall like dominos.[1] This is correct simply because of how essential eating is to life. The Lord indicates this fact by making Himself available to us as *bread*. In unfathomable love, the Almighty makes Himself truly available to us as our food — in a manner that couldn't be more vulnerable, more accessible, or more approachable. He says, "This is my body, which is given for you" (Luke 22:19).

We take a piece of this timeless love and consume it, such that God's presence enters into and transforms every part of us. We take His Body into our mouths. We swallow. We eat His Body and drink His Blood. The idea is that *we are what we eat*; that is, we are to so saturate every aspect of our body-soul union with Christ that we become His hands and feet to a kidnapped world. Yes, that which we digest holds a fundamental significance of which, I suspect, we've only scratched the surface.

Other Struggles Related to Ingestion

Gluttony isn't the only vice that functions by putting something into the body. For example, people who suffer from alcoholism, substance abuse, or any chemical dependency are, generally speaking, all ingesting something into their bodily systems. Bulimia, anorexia, and self-cutting also engage the human body very directly, as do harmful behaviors related to lust—like gluttony, a *sin of the flesh* (1 Cor. 6:12–20).

Vices related to rage, vengeance, and hatred might also be understood in relation to bodily digestion. To explain, in speaking against the harmful and addictive nature of violence, St. Augustine describes how his friend Alypius got hooked on Roman blood sport—a truly abominable form of "entertainment." Augustine laments the first time his friend attended such an event, heard the screams, and eventually peeled open his eyes to see what was happening. As Augustine describes, in *looking* at the violence, Alypius "gulped down," "drank in," and got "drunk" on the sight of it—and in doing so, suffered a wound worse than the gladiator in the arena.[2] What our eyes behold, our spirit drinks.

The Expulsion of Rational Thinking

To extend our discussion even further, all vices—regardless how closely they relate to bodily ingestion—possess the same darkening power. One of the issues that Aristotle addresses in his *Nicomachean Ethics* regards the blindness and sheer irrationality displayed by people who are lost in a vice. When people are living in the immaturity of vice, it inhibits their ability to see clearly and think coherently.[3] Naturally, then, it's especially difficult to reason about morality with a person whose immorality has rendered him *unreasonable*.

Sin and Ignorance Go Together

Whenever a person engages in vicious conduct, it attacks clarity and darkens understanding. Even though a person who is enslaved to a sin is observably miserable, he will often persist in his harmful behavior—even defend it. Through routine practice, the vice internalizes to the point that destructive choices actually feel normal to the person. His capacity to recognize his actions as harmful is thus compromised, rendering sin and ignorance — the *twofold darkness into which we were born*[4] — to be regular bedfellows. As Aristotle says,

> For when someone lacks understanding, his desire for the pleasant is insatiable and seeks indiscriminate satisfaction. The [repeated] active exercise of appetite increases the appetite he already had from birth, and if the appetites are large and intense, they actually expel rational calculation.[5]

Vice *expels rational calculation*. In other words, it hinders a person's ability to comprehend himself and his own decisions with clarity and accuracy. Vicious behavior thereby presents a conundrum: a vicious person is often not aware that he is vicious.

APPLYING THE CONCEPTS ACROSS THE BOARD

History is rife with examples of entire social groups becoming vicious and irrational in their adoption of such glaring moral problems as racism, terrorism, and genocide. Yet, we don't need to look to these grand-scale ethical dilemmas in society to understand Aristotle's observation about the blindness and absurdity of vice. Instead, we can readily see sin's insanity at a personal and daily level.

The Case of the Park Bully

I once encountered a bully in a public park who was belittling a young girl. I ran to the scene and stepped between the bully and his victim. I comforted the crying girl and encouraged her to go over to her parents. As she left, I turned to face the bully to draw his verbal fire away from the child. I calmly encouraged him to think about his actions. I said that making little girls cry is an immature and dysfunctional way for a person to try to feel better about himself, and that his behavior made him look insecure rather than powerful. I asked him whether someone had hurt his feelings, and if there were anything that I could do to help.

The bully did not thank me for illumination. On the contrary, his ears turned purple, he maniacally flailed his arms at me, and he yelled a cackle-laugh—but at least he was no longer screaming at the little girl. Of course, not everybody responds to correction by rejecting it; in fact, a wise man will receive it. "Do not reprove a scoffer, or he will hate you; reprove a wise man and he will love you" (Prov. 9:8). Again, the reality I wish to highlight from Aristotle's *Ethics* is that vice makes us blind and stupid.

My Own Blindness

As Proverbs just reminded us, the virtue of wisdom is a powerful ally against the ignorance and irrationality that vice breeds. Yet, even after an honest friend had talked to me plainly about my extreme weight gain and its dangers, I did not heed wisdom's counsel. Instead, I experienced the frightening power of vice to darken one's vision and lower one's IQ. Without a doubt, Aristotle was right—the vice of gluttony had "expelled rational calculation." I discovered firsthand how much power we surrender to the lies we tell ourselves.

Embarking on the Road to Healing

My scale reading was the blaring alarm that woke me from self-deception. I saw the problem and experienced a solemn conviction of the need to change. I went straightaway into a range of weight-loss strategies that each assured dazzling results. Although my realization of the need to change was good in and of itself, I made the mistake of running headfirst into a therapeutic world that—by handling the healing process as though it was a purely human endeavor—was dreadfully ill-equipped to the task at hand. Although certain diet and exercise tactics could be partially helpful, they could never deliver, by themselves, what they promised.

TWO

What's Lacking in the Wide World of Therapy

My First Diet

SHORTLY AFTER MY moment of enlightenment in which I realized the need to lose over a hundred pounds in order to be healthy,
I came down with a severe illness that started the process for me.
In particular, I contracted a gastrointestinal virus that ravaged my
digestive system and hospitalized me for a week. Moreover, my
weakened digestive track took the next six months to heal fully.
During that time, I was on a strict diet that prohibited white foods.

When I asked my doctor what it meant for me to avoid white
foods, she explained that the diet pretty much meant exactly what it
said. If a food or drink was white in color, then I needed to avoid it,
with the exception of bananas for which I was grateful. Rice, pasta,
potatoes, milk, cheese, and bread came in white—all of which were
off limits because of the difficulty my body would have in processing
them. Anytime that I would splurge and eat something from the
forbidden list, I would quickly pay for it with sharp stomachaches.

With the help of applesauce, hummus, and pulverized baby-food
versions of other meals from the blender, I survived the six-month
recovery. The special dietary restrictions kept me away from most
carbohydrates and dairy foods for half a year, and I thereby lost

the first fifty pounds of my hundred-pound goal—albeit against my will. But, during this time, I tasted the hope that weight loss was in fact possible for me, and I enjoyed the thrill of shopping for smaller-sized clothes.

The Weight Comes Back

Not surprisingly, however, after recovering completely from the damage done by the stomach virus, I quickly recalled the carnal ecstasies of carbs and ice cream, and I gained much of the weight back. This reversion to my old ways, my old size, and my old clothes discouraged me deeply. Feeling outright depressed and defeated by the failure, I comforted myself by binge eating. This decision resulted in even more weight gain and increased discouragement that, in turn, led to greater food consumption. It was a vicious, downward spiral; anyone who has struggled with any vice is, no doubt, familiar with such a pattern.

Other Attempts and the Same Results

I never wanted to see the number 300 on the scale again. When it came back within reach, I said to myself, "That's it. I'm going to fix this problem!" I decided to get back on the wagon with the help of a weight-loss product known as "Right-Sized Smoothie"—a supplement that I believe is no longer available. This meal replacement system was a vitamin-infused smoothie powder that used generous amounts of cinnamon and white willow bark to suppress one's appetite naturally. Blended with water or skim milk, the beverage replaced two of my meals per day while successfully curbing my hunger. And, it worked—at first; I lost ten pounds relatively quickly.

Then I got a new job and moved into a different apartment. Although this change was good news in most respects, it upset my burgeoning dietary habits. There is something so jarring about uprooting and replanting in different soil. Even when it's better ground, people—like plants—will experience an initial "wilting period" simply from the shock of the change. The move disrupted all of my established routines, and, yet again, I gained back all the weight.

I tried the smoothie diet a couple more times, but it never worked for long. Frustrated, and searching for a better system, I turned to one of my sisters again. This time, it was Shaylyn that came through. She introduced me to P-90X, an exercise routine with DVD guides that she sent to me.[1]

I installed sit-up and pull-up bars in my apartment, and I committed myself to the three-month intensive workout regime, following along and performing all the exercises. Just like the smoothie, it worked—at first. I lost over twenty pounds in only three months, but then I started preparing for my comprehensive exams while adjunct teaching for a nearby college. High anxiety levels, time constraints, and another disrupted schedule erased all my recent progress.

My next step was joining a local gym where, for a time, I worked out faithfully three times each week. But each new semester would shift my schedule and upset my exercise and dietary routine. At one point, in the middle of all of this, I hired a nutrition counselor. He opened our first session together by asking, "So, Ian, tell me about *this problem.*" He proceeded to have me track my daily food and drink consumption in a journal and prescribed a specific diet and exercise regimen. It worked—for a while.

Realizing That Something's Missing

Of course, there was nothing inherently wrong with all of these diet and exercise plans in and of themselves. Rather, my issue transcended these practices altogether; there was something else, something essential that had been missing. Whatever it was, I was never going to find it in these programs—this crucial element to healing was absent from every therapeutic avenue I'd attempted thus far.

DISCUSSION

The Wide World of Caregiving

My experience with the series of unsuccessful weight-loss strategies exemplifies a far-reaching phenomenon that plagues the whole realm of professional care. The discussion of this phenomenon is not undertaken to denigrate the countless worthy and generous souls who enter caring professions through a multitude of avenues: therapists, psychologists, counselors, doctors, ministers, advisors, spiritual directors, personal trainers, military chaplains, and so on all share the noble calling of caring for others. Essentially these heroes are called to *love*—and this is the most sublime endeavor of all. But, precisely because of the sublimity of their endeavor, their field of battle has also suffered some of the devil's most sinister and unrelenting assaults.

Deception, confusion, and incompleteness have infiltrated the realm of care such that well-meaning caregivers across a range of careers are unknowingly promoting approaches to healing that are only partially true.[2] Treatment plans that are advocated for in books and direct therapies may attempt to promote emotional healing, psychological wellness, inner tranquility, and the like, but in their limited scope they have become deficient, distorted, and even harmful—all because an indispensable truth is missing. In some cases, they are actually keeping people sick. Indeed, my own list of failed diets was but one example of this larger issue.

What the World of Caregiving Often Overlooks: Naming the Missing Piece

What exactly is the missing piece? In order to begin exploring this question and searching for its answer, it's helpful to take a second look at my failed weight-loss attempts. First, let's talk about what my various failed wellness plans didn't talk about. For instance, when my doctor detailed the no-white-food diet, she made no mention of physical exercise—yet diet and exercise naturally go hand-in-hand. Similarly, my dietitian talked about *how* to lose weight—but never said a word about *why*. The meal replacement programs and the workout videos stressed the weight problem that I was being rescued *from*—with no mention of the happiness I was being rescued *for*.

In point of fact, it wasn't just one thing that they all left out. For starters, none of these healing avenues addressed faith, which is an essential part of every human being. Neither did a single one pay so much as a passing glance to prayer. Not one covered how emotions impact thinking, nor how thinking impacts emotions. They made no mention of the power of habit—how our daily rhythms become second nature over time—which is central to the entire healing process. They didn't acknowledge the ultimate destination to which an individual's life-path is headed, nor did they recognize the role that this destination—and an individual's orientation toward or away from it—plays in whether the individual is growing or declining. They didn't describe the central part that relationships play across the healing process. Overlooking the most crucial element of all, none of them spoke of grace; they did not mention its necessity or the complete futility of my attempting to attain success by my own efforts.

Ultimately, they seemed to understand success as *getting rid of something bad,* rather than *attaining something good.* Obesity's defeat was itself the goal, as though winning meant nothing more than the other guy losing. In brief, when it came to the prospect of future victory, the entirety of the triumph flattened to the mere removal of a previous problem. Victory involved no substantial joy or abundant life in and of itself.

Whether they emphasized the body to the neglect of the mind, the physical to the neglect of the spiritual, a single moment to the neglect of long-term development, diet to the neglect of exercise, or vice versa, they were all committing the same basic error. Namely, they were all stressing only one thing, while ignoring everything else. That is, they all took one piece of the picture and treated it as though it were the whole picture—like taking one slice of bread and then confusing it for the whole loaf.

This tendency is called "reductionism" because it *reduces* the whole to just one part. It begins by deconstructing reality into its component pieces and then compartmentalizing one disconnected piece all by itself. The other parts are ignored. The connections are ignored. The big picture gets lost. In sum, the essential truth that is missing from so many reductionist approaches to caregiving is this: the *unity of reality*—the fact that all of the various parts of the world are interconnected and occur together in the whole event of living.[3] Inevitably, therapeutic avenues that totalize one disconnected piece will be incomplete at best and dangerous at worst.

How the Unity of Reality Was Forgotten

How did the wide world of caregiving lose sight of a truth as observable and essential as the unity of all reality? I blame the Enlightenment. To be fair, the Enlightenment period certainly had its good points. When it comes to the technological innovations that led to my car and my dishwasher, and when it comes to the advances in healthcare that led to the antibiotics that can make my sore throat go away, I'm a fan. In certain respects, this era did a phenomenal job of dissecting and examining the constituent facets of reality in order to accomplish unprecedented levels of illumination, understanding, and innovation. Yet, in other respects, this era dissected the different parts of reality to such a degree that it forgot to put the pieces back together again. It lost the big picture.[4]

The Tale of the Toy Firetruck

I liken the Enlightenment period to a child who takes apart his toy firetruck because he wants to better understand how it works. When the boy first deconstructs it, he is gratefully fascinated by the toymaker's creation, coming to appreciate the truck's wheels for movement, its ladder for reaching high windows, and its hose for connecting to the hydrant. After a while, however, the boy becomes arrogant. He comes to feel as though he has *mastered* the toy in his enhanced understanding of its constituent mechanisms. By alleging to have "figured it all out," his previous sense of grateful wonder is replaced by an emergent disdain. Under the illusion of mastery and control, and in increasingly and eventually utter irrationality, he even comes to view himself as the toymaker.

Whenever he sees his friends joyfully playing with their toy firetrucks, he seeks to disillusion them, teaching them how to take the toys apart. He says, "See, that's all it is." From there, some of his friends go a step further and try to take the ladder apart, while other children dismantle the wheels. Soon, there is a faction of kids claiming that the rungs of the ladder are the most important part, while another faction of children argues that the rubber of the wheels is the most significant. Both groups at least agree in making fun of that third group of kids who think that the red paint is what matters most for making it "pretty," because the red paint has nothing to do with functionality. In the end, all these groups of children have is a broken toy.

Applying the Analogy of the Toy Firetruck

In a similar way, the Enlightenment period set the stage for the deconstruction of reality into its component parts, including theology, philosophy, anthropology, psychology, and so on. To be clear, specialization itself is not the issue. Each of these disciplines provides particular competencies that we *should* honor and appreciate. To echo St. Paul's analogy in which people are the different organs of one body (1 Cor. 12:12–27; Rom. 12:4–5), all specialists ought to be respected and received for what they contribute to the whole. But, while specialized fields can add to each other and so contribute to a better understanding of the whole, losing the unity between them has proved catastrophic. The Enlightenment's excited fragmentation of reality never made a plan for putting the toymaker's creation back together again—for enjoying it as a unified whole. In this sense, it became the "Enstupidment."

This Babel-like explosion of the whole into compartmentalized fragments has, in turn, plagued the fields of professional care ever since. Theology, philosophy, anthropology, and psychology have in some cases become islands; the inherent connections between them have been forgotten. In truth, an anthropologist who ignores theology ends up with an incomplete vision of humankind—rightly understood, spirituality is an essential part of humanity. Meanwhile, a psychologist who neglects anthropology ends up with a distorted understanding of the human psyche, and theologians who disregard the contributions of psychology can find their explorations into divine mysteries to be out of touch with the daily realities of humanity. This is precisely what's happening in our culture today.

Deconstruction Continues

Dissecting practices even further within each discipline, clinicians have developed cognitive behavioral therapies for the mind, emotional exercises for the heart, medications for the brain, isometrics for the body, and communication tools for our relationships—tactics which could actually be assets, if only they could maintain a comprehensive awareness of one another and an appreciation of their inherent interconnectedness. But, worse even than ignoring each other, they rarely incorporate the foundational role of faith into their analyses. And, worst of all, the ultimate Counselor — the Holy Spirit — is ignored wholesale.[5] The resulting perspective is naturally and hopelessly skewed. Because of this distorted view, and especially because of what it leaves out, such approaches can never fully heal a human being. On the contrary, they may actually breed dysfunction.

APPLYING THE CONCEPTS ACROSS THE BOARD

Certainly, the disjointed and limited scope of my weight-loss attempts accounts for the failure of those attempts, but again, my story is merely illustrative of the larger issue we've been discussing. To demonstrate, one campus psychiatrist observed how the university that employed her "cared" for students during some of their most anxious and vulnerable moments: by supplying free condoms.[6] This alleged therapy totalized "unwanted pregnancy" as the only consideration, the only "negative" to be avoided. Meanwhile, a host of valid emotional, psychological, and spiritual factors was simply ignored—such as the anxieties of intimacy outside of committed wedlock, the severing of the unitive and procreative dimensions of human sexuality, the dignity of the unborn, and the sheer heartache that occurs in a breakup *after* bonding hormones have been released through intercourse. Trauma resulted from the heartbreak of the hook-up culture, inflicting lifelong wounds. What could the university do with all those traumatized students? Well, they could—and did—start handing out antidepressants.

The psychiatrist who was studying this mess recognized that medication could only seek to alleviate a symptom—it couldn't heal the broken person. She also rightly observed that the "platitudes, misinformation, and free condoms" offered by campus counselors were actually causing the damage in the first place.[7] Thankfully, her courageous work at this university helped to bring true healing to thousands.

Additional Examples

Equally heartbreaking cases abound, such as counselors actually advising struggling married couples to view pornography. The glaring issue of *encouraging the deadly sin of lust* is bad enough already (Matt. 5:28). Compounding the difficulty, these "caregivers" have completely ignored the biological reality of pornography's effect on the human brain: it functions similarly to an addictive opioid.[8] The notion of trying to heal relational distance between spouses by prescribing adultery and functional narcotics is absurd. But tragically, it's happening. And it's happening because important aspects of the big picture are indiscriminately disregarded.

Yet another example is "treating" an ill-tempered man by encouraging him to entertain fantasies of murdering those who have hurt him. In reality, this "therapy" fuels violence and vengeance in the heart, which is patently destructive and absolutely not healing. A more comprehensive approach, one that honors the unity of reality, would (1) validate any appropriate anger resulting from an unjust injury, then (2) guide the man in letting go of hatred, and finally, (3) lovingly accompany him across the process of forgiveness.[9] But when emotions are the *only* piece of the picture under consideration, I suppose a person could try to justify any activity that makes somebody *feel* better—even one that promotes revenge which, in truth, cuts an even deeper wound.

If, in hearing these examples of misguided "care," you've thought, "That's *crazy*," your instinct is an insightful one. Let us remember that whenever beliefs and practices "do not cohere with reality," we're dealing with the defining concept behind the terms *neurosis* and *psychosis*. By definition, neurotic behaviors regard some *distortion* of reality, and psychotic episodes regard a *break* with reality.[10] The relevant point for our discussion is that whenever misguided therapies lose the big picture, they no longer operate within an unadulterated reality. In other words, by losing the unity of reality, they *lose coherence with what is actually real*. Paradoxically, inaccurate therapeutic measures can thus perpetuate the very neuroses and psychoses that the field of therapy seeks to heal. Some of the professional advisement out there in the world today is, quite literally, insane.

Remembering the Toy Firetruck

Considering how much they left out, it's no wonder my weight-loss programs failed. By totalizing one area while overlooking the others, strategies that were meant to be for healing actually became inadequate and unsatisfying. They missed the big picture and lost sight of the connections between the different pieces. Keeping the whole "firetruck" in mind, a full healing process would include *all* of the following: the relationship between grace and healing, the constant interplay between feelings and thought processes, the inherent bond between body and spirit, the connection between habits and character formation, the link between past decisions and present predicaments, and the link between today's decisions and tomorrow's realities. No authentic or lasting healing can ever really happen except through this cohesive, holistic understanding of the human person.

THREE

A Catholic Approach to Personal Healing

Flash-Forward to Victory

THE TRAGIC EXAMPLES of misguided wellness strategies that were explored in the previous chapter might understandably leave a person feeling troubled or even angry—but this book is not a doomsday lament about the state of the world. On the contrary, this call to healing is a message of the good news, hope, and freedom found in Christ. As such, I wish to offer a motivating glimpse of my "happy ending," which, from a Catholic perspective, is actually a happy *beginning*. Namely, I am overjoyed to report that God revealed a therapeutic path that works. In the end, I lost over a hundred pounds.

Ever since that fateful moment when the button popped off my sports coat and whistled across the room, I had dreamed of losing my excess weight. Armed with the therapeutic tools outlined herein, I watched God make that dream come true. By the Lord's delivering grace, I eventually broke the 200-pound barrier; I weighed less than 200 pounds for the first time since high school. In contrast to the myriad of diet and exercise strategies that didn't work, the Catholic path to wellbeing was God's instrument for deliverance that was comprehensive and lasting. Simply put, a Catholic approach is what got me out of those old elastic stretch-slacks and into sustainable and happy health.

I struggle to find adequate words to relay what it was like for me to stand on the scale some time ago and see the new number light up. It didn't read 303, nor the seemingly never-ending 250 where I'd been stuck for years. Instead, I was over a century of weight down from where I began. Where I once kicked my scale aside in frustration, now I just stood there and stared at it, as a swell of gratitude rendered me speechless.

In whatever area of life you seek healing, I wish this same joy for you. Whatever the need is, the power you will encounter in the Great Physician is sufficient to the task ahead. As you encounter the life-saving truths of the Gospel throughout the remainder of this journey, I encourage you to give Jesus a chance. Trust the process—if you take up your cross daily, die to self, and abide in Him, then healing is inevitable because of *who He is*. I also encourage you to take your own testimony of Christ's victory and share it with anyone who needs to hear some good news.

DISCUSSION

Losing the Unity of Reality at a Personal Level

The dissection of reality into disconnected, splintered fragments doesn't just affect the world of ideas. It affects the way we live our daily lives. Many of us struggle as we live the various aspects of our daily existence in disconnected compartments, split apart into separate pieces—just as the Enlightenment split apart the academic disciplines. Our faith-life takes place on an island that is isolated from our work-life. Virtue disappears at the sports stadium without a second thought. Web browsing bears no resemblance to spiritual convictions. Road rage ends as family time begins. Once, during Mass, I found myself sincerely offering the sign of peace to the same sister-in-Christ whom I had cut off for a better parking space earlier the same morning. Even if that day's homily had been about valuing others above oneself (Phil. 2:3), I likely still wouldn't have recognized the contradiction.

Parking-lot conversation, social media posting, dinner selection, and texting can seem like different television stations as we switch from one to the next, perhaps feeling like a different person in each scenario. We'll go from gossip to the Golden Rule and then back again, without hesitation. We know that beatitude matters, we know that work responsibilities are significant, and we realize that how we spend our money is important—but each area of life remains isolated on its own channel, separate from the others. We tend to lose sight of how, in truth, they're all tethered together.

A Few Telling Examples

During his morning devotional time, a Catholic man reads Scriptures about how all are equal in Christ (Gal. 3:28) and how "God shows no partiality" (Rom. 2:11–16; Acts 10:34) — and he agrees wholeheart-edly. Yet, throughout the afternoon, anxious thoughts and resulting insecurities revolve around famous people with money, power, and material possessions. He starts to feel like a nobody in contrast to individuals whom the kingdom of this world deems well-known, high profile, or influential — based upon this world's backward standards of importance. It's as though the biblical assurances of equal human dignity and worth that he'd read earlier are entirely disconnected from the rest of his day. Despite his earlier Scripture study, he still has no idea how irreplaceably precious he is to God. How does this happen?

A woman genuinely believes in free will, but she feels trapped by the tendency to be unsympathetic toward her daughter — a tendency she inherited from her own mom. One day, when her daughter tries to open up about a struggle at school, this woman reflexively snaps back in a cold tone of voice, telling her child to "get over it." When the young girl asks her mother to show a little more compassion, the woman replies in frustration, "Well, I was born and raised like this. It's just who I am. Take it or leave it, because there's nothing I can do about it. I can't change. I'm stuck this way." To be clear, this mother has fallen prey to the reductionist lie of *determinism*, which denies free will under the false claim that people's "decisions" are totally predetermined by nature and nurture.[1] And yet, she still says that she believes in human freedom and even attempts to teach it to her daughter — although she just stated the opposite. In reality, people are certainly *influenced* by genetics and upbringing, no doubt, but we are not *predetermined* by them. God gave us the gift of free will; we can *choose* to change such that there will be "a new creation: everything old has passed away; see, everything has become new!" (2 Cor. 5:17). So, we ask ourselves, how did this mother unwittingly ascribe to determinism?

When I was a Baptist minister, I once preached a sermon about vice. I read Bible verses about it — such as Titus 1:10–12, 2 Timothy

3:1–9, and Galatians 5:19–21; these provide lists of various vices and descriptions of their destructive impact. Relevant to my own weakness, these accounts named gluttony alongside hatred, lying, and witchcraft. In a subsequent sermon, not long after, I boasted about how many fattening cheeseburgers I'd eaten that week, and I did so without a second thought. I didn't recognize the blatant incompatibility between these two proximate messages that I'd delivered to my congregation. Again, we ask ourselves, how can such an unknowing contradiction occur?

It happens because vice makes us blind, as observed earlier. It also happens because human lives have become fractured into disjointed compartments. To put it simply, neither I nor that mother nor that man with his morning devotionals connected the dots. Switching channels from one separate partition of existence to the next, we all completely missed the harmful elements in our life and outlook that were blocking us from right understanding and happiness. These unseen destructive forces within us can become the most dangerous of all — precisely because they're unseen. This is exacerbated by the fact that we have a real enemy who prefers to operate unnoticed and unchallenged. (Remember that Tolkien's *evil* ring of power renders its wearer *invisible*.[2]) In brief, we tend to think and behave in isolated compartments and overlook the big picture — and in doing so, we can miss what matters most. Like the architects of today's world of caregiving, we have lost sight of the union of reality. If we truly wish to heal, we need it back.

The Question of the Hour

So, we have the answer — in theory. But, is there actually holistic care out there? Is there a therapeutic strategy available that illumines a larger view? One that can cast revealing light on our personal demons — both figurative and literal — so they can no longer run about unchecked and unchallenged, wreaking havoc? Is there a comprehensive approach to wellness that reconnects the splintered fragments of therapy, thereby helping us to reconnect the broken pieces of ourselves? Yes, there is. But you won't find it in secular self-help books.

Clinical Research Today: Strides and Limitations

While a number of scholars have recognized the tendency toward fragmentation and are working to restore a more comprehensive approach, glaring oversights continue to contaminate the world of care. Atheistic denials of transcendent realities have left an indelible mark upon the mental health professions, as have utilitarian views that stress usefulness over dignity.[3] And Hellenistic roots run deep; psychology still echoes ancient schools of thought that emphasized the mere *reduction of suffering* rather than the *attainment of abundant life*.[4] All of these influences work against the unity of reality by promoting shortsighted perspectives in some way or another. Coupled with the affinity for disintegration inherited from the Enlightenment, contemporary therapy still struggles to embrace a view of reality that is complete and accurate.

Even where "positive psychologists" are taking welcomed steps toward a bigger picture, their methods still fall short to the extent that they omit faith.[5] That is, their work cannot go as far as what a full union of faith and reason makes possible.[6] Refreshingly, some secular scholars identify that something "transcendent" is definitely at work in human lives, and they can even observe that it "summons" us.[7] Yet, this observable transcendence remains anonymous—the "transcendent summoner" has no name. Sadly, they overlook the fact that the Divine has revealed Himself, His love, and His Name to His creation so that we could know Him. To the extent that they neglect what the Creator has revealed, their contributions remain correspondingly and inevitably limited. Is there some good to be found, received, and appreciated from the realm of secular care? Absolutely. But it won't come close to the healing power available in God's Christ.

Moving Beyond the Limitations

In the final analysis, approaches to healing born out of piecemeal, limited, and distorted worldviews gravitate toward the alleviation of pain, the treatment of symptoms, and the solving of problems. But what of substantial happiness, beyond the mere riddance of negatives? God has in fact given us a few maps that chart the transcendent and otherwise unseen regions of reality—we are wise to follow them. In other words, only the Creator's self-disclosure offers us the fullest possible picture of the world. Therefore, only God's revelation offers the best possible understanding of what healing is, what it is we're healed from, and, more importantly, what it is we're healed *for*. And only God's grace makes real healing achievable.

The Catholic Worldview Embraces the Unity of Reality

Contrary to the limitations and distortions of reductionism, Christianity presents an interconnected view of *every* aspect of creation. I'm reminded that the word "catholic" literally means *universal*, the *whole* picture. The Catholic worldview, based upon the Creator's self-revelation in Christ, recognizes the entire natural world as God's creation. It acknowledges the wondrous, vast array of various parts that make up the whole, and it honors the interwoven nature of all these components. Most exciting of all is that, as Catholics, we get to bear witness to that transcendent territory which, for many people, remains uncharted and anonymous.

Applying St. Paul's Imagery

What I appreciate so much about Paul's analogy of the Church as a body is that he not only describes us as different bodily organs interconnected and dependent upon one another, but even *present within one another*. In the human body, the cardiovascular system includes, within it, oxygen receptors to receive from the respiratory system; at the same time, the respiratory system contains, within it, capillaries for receiving the blood supply of the cardiovascular system. This bodily imagery thus illustrates a profound reality: each component piece of the whole is both *distinct* and *part of* the other pieces—all at the same time. The constitutive parts of the whole are actually *present within* one another.

As Paul's analogy conveys, the *Catholic* worldview is by definition a *universal* understanding of the whole. It recognizes that the insights of different specialists are connected parts of the same body, and it appreciates how these parts are present within one another. As Benedict XVI says,

> The Church's social doctrine, which has "an important interdisciplinary dimension," can exercise, in this perspective, a function of extraordinary effectiveness. It allows faith, theology, metaphysics and science to come together in a collaborative effort in the service of humanity.[8]

An accurate worldview maintains this unified view of the whole and avoids collapsing the entire "loaf" into just one disconnected "slice." This holistic perspective, in turn, has direct ramifications for avoiding piecemeal therapy and attaining healing that is substantial, thorough, and lasting.

Healing within a Universal Framework

What exactly does the process of healing look like when we reconnect the pieces and appreciate all of the interwoven factors involved in human wellbeing? While I'll answer that over the course of this entire book, for now, I'll highlight seven interlocking pillars upon which this exploration is built. (1) First, a Catholic approach focuses on the person, not the problem. In particular, it focuses primarily upon the three Persons of the Holy Trinity and, subsequently, upon the dignified human person made in His image. Because it's grounded upon God, love will be central—as will relationships with God and neighbor. Similarly, the *natural law*, God's way of love inscribed onto humanity, will also be central.

From there, (2) a Catholic method will recognize the necessity of the Creator's grace in healing His creation. Thus, it will realize our needs for humility, prayer, and acquiescence to the daily guidance of the Holy Spirit. It will reject wholesale the lie that our own understanding and effort can save us. Rather, it will recognize our own poverty of resources—such as not having enough money, time, or skill—as blessed reminders of our radical dependency upon the Great Physician, apart from whom we cannot heal. Returning repeatedly to the fact that the healing process is all grace, the Catholic approach ever assures us that the Redeemer's mercy is bigger than the sin.[9]

In addition, (3) a Catholic path to healing could never be strictly theoretical because, in the union of nature and grace, every truth encountered will manifest in very practical, down-to-earth ways. In other words, it won't shy away from the messy, lived-out grit of it all. Rather, a Catholic framework will suggest hands-on measures for moving forward. Along the way, it will address the challenge of the Cross, the reality of constant stumbling, and the impossibility of saving ourselves. And, it will do so without inducing fear, based on the reality that the entire process remains rooted in the love of our sovereign God.

Furthermore, (4) a Catholic methodology will engage every phase of human development including daily actions, long-term habits, and a transformed character. Across this graced formation process, it will never collapse down to just one piece of our personhood. Instead of totalizing our bodily aspects or totalizing our spiritual aspects, it will recognize both parts of us—appreciating their interplay as well as their union throughout each stage of the developmental process.

In the unity of reality, (5) a Catholic perspective will cover a host of "both-ands" in what are, on the surface, divergent or contradictory elements of our nature and participation in God's creation. It will address both body and soul, both virtue and vice, both feelings and thought processes, both freedom and influence, both abundant life and redemptive suffering. It will simultaneously address the whole human condition: the inherent goodness of our having been created in God's image, the reality that we're fallen through sin, and the fact that redemption is available, all at the same time.[10] And because this comprehensive perspective understands God's creation as a unified whole, a Catholic approach will welcome the insights of science, psychology, biology, anthropology, and so forth into its therapeutic analyses.

Moreover, (6) a Catholic approach to healing will never restrict itself to a single moment in time; rather, it will examine the entire trajectory of human formation. The Catholic mindset is concerned with both the present moment and the ultimate end to which our lives are oriented, recognizing that the implications of our present actions don't stop with today. Rather, our actions—virtuous or sinful—compel us forward toward one end or another. Thus, a Catholic view looks at both *the right now* and *what we're ordered to*, both *the moment* and *our development*, both who we *are* and who we are *becoming*.

In the end, (7) a Catholic approach to human healing won't stop at the negatives we're saved from. But, more important, it will propel us forward into the positive and substantial life that we're saved for, including inner wholeness, relational growth, friendship, wonder, leisure, joy, hope, peace, and more—onward into saintly happiness we cannot yet imagine. God willing, this book—an exploration into human healing—will do justice to all of these interconnected pillars.

An Important Word about the Definition of Words

Building upon these pillars, a Catholic approach will define certain terms differently than the kingdom of this world does. For instance, a Catholic worldview understands "freedom" not as our being *free from authority* but as our being *free to be our best self*.[11] Similarly, Catholicism will define "healing" beyond the *removal of a negative*. In the unity of reality, healing is more fully understood as *God's repairing of the image that truly defines the human being*. In this same vein, when the kingdom of this world preaches, "Be true to yourself," its oversimplifications forget to distinguish between the *disordered self* and the *well-ordered self*. Healing regards being true to your *true self*, i.e., your self that is made in God's image. In contrast, being true to your broken and disordered self will only bring more destruction.

The phrase "personal healing" is also an interesting one. In the common vernacular, it comes across as indicative of something very private and individualistic. If I heard somebody say that he was reading a book about *personal healing*, I would suspect a solo endeavor—that's what the phrase has typically come to mean. But, through the lens of Catholicism, the phrase "personal healing" could never designate a purely individual experience.

Strictly grammatically, "personal healing" refers literally to *the healing of the person*—and from a Catholic perspective, the person is a fundamentally relational being that reflects the Trinitarian Community of Being. Created in the image of this Loving Relationship, persons are relational right from the start; therefore, healing could never be a purely individual experience in the first place. I would go so far as to say that anytime a caregiver is treating a person, the caregiver is simultaneously treating the person's relationships. Keeping the union of reality in mind, a complete and accurate conception of "personal healing," by definition, must coincide with "relational healing."

In a couple of cases, popular misconceptions have painted otherwise perfectly good language in a touch-feely color that is as unfortunate as it is off-putting. The term "self-care," in reality, refers to a powerful virtue rooted in our relationality as reflections of the Trinity; the Thomistic ethicist, Fr. James Keenan, goes so far as to argue that self-care should be considered among the cardinal virtues.[12] Yet, in some circles, this term has come to evoke images of nothing more than relaxing to your favorite soap opera while sipping a nightcap.

Likewise, the notion of "making friends with our feelings" — used later in this book — will refer to a robust, concrete, and thorough conception of friendship that is rooted in covenant; not to a mere playground powwow. In other words, the forthcoming imagery of *befriending our emotions* will symbolize all the rigor and wrestling inherent to forging any authentic friendship; within a Catholic framework, the idea could never be reducible to something superficial. For anyone who shares my distaste for pedestrian counterfeits, rest assured that the healing approaches discussed in this book always refer to substantial and comprehensive realities — never to fluffy misperceptions.

And now, we come to that tricky term: self-help. From everyday usage and today's reductionist emphasis on individualism, the very idea of a self-help book could understandably sound selfish. But, within a Catholic framework for healing, self-help is not a solo endeavor — nor could it be. In light of the interdependence of the various organs within the one mystical body of Christ, the healing of a self is already the healing of a community.

Harkening back to humanity's original wound, Satan lied to the first people by suggesting that God was selfishly withholding something good from them (Gen. 3:4). In short, the enemy attacked their view of God. Since people were made in God's image, this attack upon their understanding of God was simultaneously an attack on self-image. To this day, fallen humanity still misunderstands what the self actually is. If we properly understood ourselves as beloved reflections of perfect Love, then self-help could never mean self-centered.

Your Vision of Victory

Envision, if you will, what your life would look like if the area where you most desire healing received the victory you seek. I got to see myself back in regular-sized clothes and was silenced by gratitude; what does healing look like for you? Do you see sobriety and vitality where there was once addiction? Do you see serenity and joy replacing a painful memory that used to replay in your head like a broken record? A fulfilling work environment instead of an acidic and draining atmosphere? Or, do you see the power to remain self-controlled in your communication — even when your emotions are momentarily comprised? Whatever you envision, I encourage you to keep this motivating picture close to your heart as we proceed. Visualize it often, latch onto it, hold it close, and protect it. Remember: within a Catholic approach to healing, your vision isn't a fantasy. It's where you're headed. In Christ, it's something to look forward to.

A Powerful Way to Evangelize

As Catholic Christians, we possess the incomprehensible gift of having access to the fullest healing available. Perhaps one of the most effective ways we can spread the good news that our Lord has given us is by experiencing it for ourselves. When we do, we are imbued with the ability to bear witness to the larger reality that is so often overlooked. By experiencing God's healing for ourselves, we move beyond all the ideological debates. Surpassing every earthly argument, we become living proof of the Great Physician's power to save. Then, simply by watching us, our neighbors can see for themselves that the Lord is real—and that the Lord is good.

PART II

LAYING
THE CORRECT
FOUNDATION

FOUR

The Right Starting Point

THE LAST CHAPTER opened with a flash-forward to victory. But, how did I get there? Before this motivating glimpse into the future, we'd last left off my story with a list of failed diets, with each weight-loss stride quickly followed by my putting all the pounds back on. Diet and exercise are indeed critical to self-care, and inevitably, I'd have to engage these practices in order to get healthy. But these attempts hadn't taken hold. Why not? The fact is, my issue transcended these attempts altogether into something beyond the matter of simple weight loss. There was something fundamental, something vital, that had been overlooked by the myopic methods thus far. I was about to find this something in a more integrated approach that, refreshingly, embraced the unity of reality—and all the necessary healing ingredients that flow from it.

An Enlightening Role-Play

In one of my adjunct teaching assignments, I had the privilege to observe, advise, and participate in role-plays between first-year counseling students and professional Christian therapists. Each student was assigned a character to play during the mock counseling sessions, while the counselors demonstrated therapeutic practice. During one of these exercises, I witnessed an exchange that gave me language for the essential, transcendent, and crucial ingredient that

I'd been missing; it showed me what I needed first and foremost to face my issues from the right starting point.

In this particular interchange, the student played the part of a wife who was struggling both with a serious communication breakdown in her marriage and with feelings of neurotic guilt. The first half of the dialogue between the counselor and the student was a standard instructional exercise that demonstrated informational intake, open-ended questions to build the therapeutic relationship, and paraphrasing in order to show empathetic listening to clients. After these steps had been covered, the dialogue took an unexpected turn that enlightened everyone present.

"So, how can I fix this communication breakdown with my spouse? How can I solve the problem of all this guilt I'm experiencing? Please help!"

"It took a lot of courage for you to come in here today," said the therapist. "Can you think of another virtue you see in yourself?"

The student looked stunned by the question. It was clearly not what she had expected to hear, and her facial expression broke character for a moment. I was also jolted by the counselor's question; it was not what I had expected to hear either. Intrigued by the direction the therapist had taken, I listened intently, wondering where he was going with this.

After some hesitation, the student eventually answered, "Well, I've always been a naturally kind person. I have a lot of compassion for people, so I guess I'd have to say, kindness? Yeah, that's a quality that I like about myself."

The counselor replied, "Kindness is an amazing virtue. I definitely see that characteristic in you, in addition to courage. Now, I'd also like to get a better grasp on what makes you happy. Would you mind sharing what you are most grateful for in life?"

Again, with a puzzled expression on her face, the student seemed to be momentarily pulled out of the role-play. Snapping back into character, she replied, "Our two children. I'm most grateful for our children."

"Give me an example of a happy memory with your children for which you feel especially thankful," said the counselor.

The student looked a little confused, but maintained her poise. She responded, "There was this one Christmas where we got everything right! After our son unwrapped the skateboard he'd been hoping for, he ran over and gave his daddy this giant hug of unfiltered joy. I wanted to hang onto that moment, and make memories like that over and over again."

"Sounds like a truly beautiful day," said the therapist. "Let's tie that into something you mentioned earlier. I think you said that your husband used to be the man of your dreams. Can you describe what about him made him your dream guy?"

Still clearly uncertain about where the therapist was heading, she answered, "He was my dream guy for so many reasons. He made me laugh. I mean, every single day, he made me laugh. And he was such a good listener. I could tell he really cared about me when we talked. We also had a lot of interests in common. And, well, he's always been so handsome ... so many reasons."

Finally, she couldn't resist inquiring about the unexpected path that the therapeutic dialogue had taken. Staying in character, she asked the counselor, "When do we start solving my problems? I'd really like to focus on the communication and guilt issues I brought up initially. When do we get to that?"

The therapist replied, "Sounds like these struggles are a heavy burden on you right now, and it seems as though you're eager to resolve them?"

"That's right."

The therapist continued, "The reason I asked what virtue you see in yourself, what you're most grateful for, for your favorite memories, and for your most beloved qualities you see in your husband is to center this entire care process on you, your relationships, and your happiness. So much therapy today centers upon problem-solving. However, *you are not a problem to be solved.* You are a human person, with an inviolable dignity that ought never to be trespassed, with the potential for greatness, and with a divine summons upon you to prosper abundantly! We will certainly talk about healing the communication in your marriage in the course of our sessions together. However, that healing begins by looking at the marriage itself as a substantial reality of love, not by looking at its communication troubles in isolation. You also desire to get rid of unwarranted guilt, and we'll certainly talk about that, too. But merely getting rid of negatives is not enough. We also want to experience the presence of positives!"

With all eyes glued on him, he concluded, "In other words, our sessions are about you prospering in excellence, happiness, and freedom as the best version of yourself—not just getting rid of problems. If all you do is get rid of negatives, don't be surprised when other, worse problems move in to take their place. You see, the *problem* is not our foundation, because you are never reducible to a mere problem to be fixed. Instead, the basis of this entire therapy is *you*, as an inherently relational and innately dignified human being intended to flourish in life to the fullest! *That's* our starting point. It is not the problem, but the substantial reality of you, your inherent worth, the loves in your life, and your call to ultimate happiness that will ground this therapy."

The student completely broke character at this point and exclaimed a jaw-dropped, "Wow!" I saw astonished expressions across the room of students. Clearly, I was not alone in having experienced this revelation as a conversion-level epiphany: *we all have a fallen tendency to start by treating a person's problem as though it is the essence of that person.*

Processing the Epiphany

After the exercise, we reflected on this fallen tendency to reduce caring for others to mere problem-solving, without any real thought to the beloved person beneath the dysfunction. We realized how frequently the negative hijacks our focus—in professional care settings, in our everyday communication with others, and in our own self-image. We admitted that we sometimes merely pay doctrinal lip service to the reality that God created each person in His own image and likeness; we actually live as though evil has the upper hand. Together, we recognized a marked difference between being able to quote the truth that all people were made in God's image versus truly treating one another and ourselves according to this central reality.

One of my students displayed a particularly beautiful and repentant turn inward. He said, "As a Catholic, I have always believed that everybody reflects God's likeness. But, to be honest, I don't always treat people that way. I remember reading the anointed words of a Jewish rabbi. He said, 'When another person comes toward me, my attitude should be this: step aside in reverence! Behold, here approaches the image of God.' I don't always view my neighbor that way. I don't view myself that way."

Moved by his authenticity, the day's lesson internalized within me even more deeply. Countless scenarios came to mind as I ran through my mental rolodex of memories. Time and again, I realized I was falling short of the mark. When checking out at the grocery store, did I view the attendant as though he showed me the face of Jesus? Or was he just a means to an end—a man who needed to process my payment so I could carry on with my busy day? Did I even take a brief moment to thank him? Did he leave his encounter with me sensing that I felt *honored* to have been in his presence? Did he leave his encounter with me sensing Christ's love for him through me? *Was I Jesus to him?* How about the server at the restaurant when she messed up my order—did I see God's reflection in her? Or was she a problem to be solved?

DISCUSSION

In God's Image: An Examination of Conscience

When it comes to the truths of the Catholic faith, it's not that believers don't know how to recite them. Rather, the real issue is that we so often fail to abide in them. The notion that all people possess inherent dignity because they were made in God's image is quite familiar to the Christian ear. We know philosophically and theoretically that, underneath any disorder, there is a person who was created in the image and likeness of God. We know that beneath any dysfunction is a person who reflects God's love, a person who thereby possesses a sacredness not to be trespassed, an inherent and inviolable ("never violate-able") dignity. But, do we really live as though that's the case?

Beyond any classroom exercise, how many of us in our daily interactions with friends, family, and coworkers treat whatever problems we see as primary, never affirming these problem-burdened individuals as inherently dignified human beings? How many of our prayers reduce people to the difficulty we're praying about? Honestly, do we see the face of Jesus in our neighbor? Finally, turning the lens inward, do we reduce ourselves to mere problems to be fixed? Or do we live in a way that demonstrates our belief that all of us have been designed after God's own image? This is the basis of human dignity; it is because of this that we are innately good.[1] If we can believe this, we will have true joy:

> Joy. Where does it come from? How is it to be explained? Certainly, there are many factors at work here. But in my view, the crucial one is this certainty, based on faith: I am

wanted; I have a task in history; I am accepted; I am loved.... This sense of being accepted comes in the first instance from other human beings. But all human acceptance is fragile. Ultimately we need a sense of being accepted unconditionally. Only if God accepts me, and I become convinced of this, do I know definitively: it is good that I exist.[2]

Designed for Loving Relationships — Human and Divine

The origin of our creation in the image of God also means that we're meant for relational love, for, as a Trinity, God is relational—and God is love.[3] To put it simply, we were made in the image of friendship.

[T]he creation accounts in Genesis make it clear that man is not created as an isolated individual ... God placed the first human beings in relation to one another, each with a partner of the other sex. The Bible affirms that man exists in relation with other persons, with God, with the world, and with himself. According to this conception, man is not an isolated individual but a person—an essentially relational being.[4]

As Pope St. John Paul II states:

Man cannot live without love. He remains a being that is incomprehensible for himself, his life is senseless, if love is not revealed to him, if he does not encounter love, if he does not experience it and make it his own, if he does not participate intimately in it.[5]

While we can rest assured that we are creatures designed for love in our myriad human relationships, an even deeper sense of our inherent worth can be realized when we remember the fundamental loving relationship that defines each one of us: the love that God has for every particular person. In fact, "God shows no partiality"

(Rom. 2:11). The Lord pursues each individual with unfathomable love. According to God, all people were worth the ultimate sacrifice, whether they personally accept the gift or not. God's love is so personal and intimate that He knows the number of hairs on every person's head (Luke 12:7). When I really think about this fact, it staggers my mind with breathless awe and fills my heart with grateful wonder. The number of hairs on my head? *I* don't know that. It means God knows me better than I know myself! I am *known*; I am *loved*; it is *good* that I exist. Our Creator—in His joyous, particular, and immeasurable love—is the real starting point for healing. The inherent dignity that the imprint of God's love bestows upon each of us defines our core. This—and not sin—is our foundation.

Replacing a Problem-Solving Focus with the Right Starting Point

As we keep seeing, many of today's approaches reduce the healing process to fixing problems, to the elimination of a negative, to mere symptom-management. I witnessed this tendency in my first nutrition counselor when he said, "So, Ian, tell me about this problem," and subsequently treated my problem as the center of his entire therapy. It seemed as though the counselor wasn't treating *me*—his real client was the dysfunction itself.

While it is good to identify disorder, it is even more important to identify God's image underneath it. They say that the first step to healing is "admitting you have a problem." I say that the first step is realizing that you are the cherished creation of the Living God, lovingly knit together in His own image. It is only with the assurance of God's love that we have the courage to shed real light on our dreadful need.

The right starting point for healing will keep God and His image central within us, rather than making the negative our basis. One practical way we can do this is by saying the following line silently to ourselves whenever we interact with another person: "Right now, I'm looking at the image of God." We would also do well to sometimes say this line when we look in the mirror.

By leaving behind the problem-solving platform and replacing it with the truth of innate human dignity, we actually abide in the truth. Instead of paying lip service to it while living as though something else were true, we actively participate in the beautiful reality of our creation *imago Dei*. We recognize that the person, not the problem, is the center of the healing process. The three Divine Persons of the Trinity and the dignified human person crafted in God's image are what ground the entire healing process upon a foundation of love, happiness, freedom, and a fulfilling life!

The Trouble with a Presence of Absence

On a practical level, a problem-solving focus isn't only false—because it's untrue, it also *doesn't work*. As long as I treated the sin as central, I was not going to experience sustained success in my battle against obesity. The back-and-forth undulation of my seesawing addictive tendencies reminded me of the following passage from Scripture:

> When the unclean spirit has gone out of a man, he passes through waterless places seeking rest, but he finds none. Then he says, 'I will return to my house from which I came.' And when he comes he finds it empty, swept, and put in order. Then he goes and brings with him seven other spirits more evil than himself, and they enter and dwell there; and the last state of that man becomes worse than the first. (Matt. 12:43–45a; *see also*, Luke 11:24–26)

As nature abhors a vacuum, any *presence of absence* inevitably becomes an *occupied space* once again.

Regarding my obesity, whenever I would "get rid of the problem" by losing weight, it was like sweeping out an interior room and leaving it empty. Whatever evil spirits were involved in my temptations would indeed come back in larger numbers. To illustrate, each time that I cycled back to weight gain after tasting short-term success, feelings of depression and temptations to despair would accompany vice's return. An empty room was not going to work. I couldn't just "get rid of a negative." I would not know victory until I filled the space with something substantial—a firm grasp upon who Christ is and who I was in Christ.

APPLYING THE CONCEPTS ACROSS THE BOARD

The truths conveyed in this chapter are universal and essential; they are definitely not unique to gluttony. In whatever area of life you seek healing, it is vital for you to know *who you are*. You are not a problem to be fixed. You are God's beloved. You are not an ill temper, you are not a drug addiction, and you are not a burden. You are not a bad spouse, you are not a bad parent, and you are not a bad person. *You are God's beloved*. You are not a problem. You *have* a problem — which is infinitely different from *being* one. And, your Maker has made healing available to whomever wants it.

An Invitation

An intellectual awareness of what Scripture says is not enough. We must receive these truths deep into our hearts: the Almighty God calls *me* His beloved, calls *me* His bride, and calls *me* the very temple where He dwells. Do we allow this trembling truth to penetrate into the deepest places of our interior, where it needs to saturate us? Do we allow ourselves to be searched and known by God, knowing that He sees all, accepting that we are forgiven, and allowing Him to love us in that vulnerable state? Do we recognize His image in ourselves, and so see our own innate dignity? Or, do we understand ourselves primarily as a problem?

I ask you to take a moment to invite God into your heart. Take a moment to let Him see you fully as you are, both the dysfunction and the inherently dignified reflection of Himself that rests underneath. Ponder, listen, and be filled with wonder. Taking joy in God is a two-way street — as you take joy in the Lord, He takes joy in you. So, use this moment to silence your hurried thoughts, and allow the Bridegroom to take delight in His bride. Pray together with Augustine, "Within me was a hunger of that inward food, Yourself, my God."[6] Pray with David, "Search me, O God, and know my heart" (Ps. 139:23). Allow yourself to be loved. Really *let God love you*. Know that you are not a problem to be fixed. Take rest in the truth that you are beloved, pursued, and delighted in. Think about the awesome fact that God awaits you.

FIVE

Mother of All Virtue

The Laying of a New Foundation Continues

LONG BEFORE I had the particular language of understanding that I shared in the last chapter, God had already revealed to me the reality that I am not fundamentally a problem. It was through the Rite of Christian Initiation of Adults (RCIA) that He introduced me to these beautiful truths. Granted, my grasp of these ideas was still incomplete; yet, during the year leading up to my entry into the Church, an emphasis upon the dignity of the human person started to replace an emphasis upon evil.

By moving away from a misplaced focus on the negative and grounding my efforts instead upon God's love, I had taken my first step into a larger world—one in which sustainable healing was possible. Yet, it was only the first step. I still wasn't ready to dive directly into the healthy habits of self-care; a more foundational virtue was needed first. Just as God had opened me up to the ineffectiveness of problem-solving approaches to weight loss, He also enlightened me to my dire need for humility.

Humiliation Brings Humility

This much-needed epiphany happened at a graduate-school conference—held sometime during the year that I was enrolled in RCIA—when a very famous, world-renowned speaker gave the colloquium's keynote address. All anybody would have seen looking at me that particular evening was a professional graduate student of theology, feverishly attentive, taking notes, and appearing eager to grow deeper in my faith. What was actually happening inside of me was quite a different story.

Despite my attempts to appear studious and confident, I actually felt intimidated by the speaker's success. I felt as though I was *worth less* than he was because, unlike him, the world didn't know who I was—I felt *worthless*. I also felt envious. The entire experience was miserable. The only thing on my mind was, in some way, to get the crowd's attention on me and impress the girl sitting next to me.

When the speaker opened the floor for public question-and-answer time, my hand was the first to go up. I said, "Sir, you stated earlier that St. Augustine tells us that 'all truth is God's truth.' That's one of my favorite quotes, but I believe this idea originally comes from Clement of Alexandria."

He replied, "I'm pretty sure Augustine says that."

"But Clement said it first," I retorted, then sat back down.[1] I felt my nerves calm down because all eyes were on me, and everybody was now aware that I knew something the speaker didn't. "I must look so cool to the girl sitting next to me," I thought to myself, although her face said otherwise. In the classic blindness of vice, I didn't yet realize that I had just advertised my narcissism to the whole assembly and so embarrassed myself.

God's enlightenment came the following weekend when, over a game of chess with one of my professors, he talked about the incident. He told me that the speaker was a friend of his, and that he had spoken with him privately after the keynote about how disheartened he felt when, after working so hard on giving the university a message worth hearing, somebody in attendance tried to upstage him in front of everyone. After describing the speaker's hurt feelings to me in detail, my professor said, "Yeah, some know-it-all needed everybody to know that a quotation the speaker cited may have had an earlier source in Clement's thought … I wasn't able to be there, but I sure hope he wasn't referring to you. That wasn't you, was it?" I told him it wasn't me.

Facing the Arrogance and Fear Within

After lying to my professor, which I also needed to confess, I did some painful soul-searching about my motives during the event's Q & A. I saw the pride and the envy fueling my remarks. I saw that I wasn't comfortable in my own skin. I recognized that I often adopted the role of the critic because I'd rather be the one doing the critiquing than the one being criticized. In short, I realized a sobering truth about myself: I was arrogant.

I also recognized that fear lay beneath the arrogance. Forgetting God's infinite love for me, I was afraid that I didn't matter. I realized that I sought my sense of self-worth in the approval of other people rather than in God's love for me. I saw that this idol was making me miserable, wasn't true, and was entirely unnecessary. I realized that my criticism had no love in it — it was self-serving rather than being motivated by a desire to serve others. It was for me, not for the speaker. Fear had been blocking me from the freedom of love.

Performance Reviewer versus Grateful Recipient

One of the fastest ways to appear better than your neighbor is to position yourself as a *critical evaluator*. In my case, this always-giving-never-receiving critical posture — a condition that a friend of mine calls "young man's disease" — was based not in love but in pride. I'd later know firsthand how obnoxious it feels for a speaker to pick up a heckler in the crowd; I cringe looking back at my old self. I recognize today that I used to be *that guy*, heckling the speaker because of my own insecurity and arrogance—two faces of the same sin.

In short, I wasn't receiving from others. I was like an organ of the body bent on giving the other organs what I had to offer, but starving because I wouldn't allow their life supplies into myself. God opened my eyes to how I'd been orienting myself toward the world around me—as always trying—through self-importance—to be the one doing the giving. I saw that this pretense of selflessness hid a deep-seated, sinful hubris. I never would have said it out loud so baldly, but my actions and attitudes were saying it: "I have it all sorted out. Everyone else is in need of what I have to offer. You have nothing to offer me because I'm not the one in need. I have arrived." This is the message communicated by a *refusal to receive*. What horrified me most was how I'd been abiding in the worst kind of sin possible—the spiritual pride that many of the religious leaders of Jesus' day exhibited—all while living immersed in church work.

While listening to homilies or conference talks, my questions were, "How do I evaluate the job being done by the speaker? Did he commit any accidental heresies? How could I deliver the same message better? What comment might I make afterward to appear knowledgeable or get people's eyes on me? How can I get a chance to speak at this event?" My questions were not, "What do I need from the Lord through my brother? How can this message help me realize where I need to repent? How do I see Christ's image in the speaker? What do I appreciate most about this other person?" My lack of receiving manifested itself in the following way: I treated the world around me as though it was being presented to me for my critical assessment. That is, I postured myself toward the world in the self-proclaimed role of *performance reviewer* rather than *grateful recipient*.

A Fable to Illustrate My Condition

A fan of fantasy, especially the stories of Tolkien and the allegories of Lewis, I appreciate the power of fiction to express truth in a creative way. Accordingly, I imagined a brief allegorical parable of my own, which expresses my lesson at the colloquium better than any straightforward explanation could. I envisioned a fable about Kridic the Pale Dwarf—a renowned food critic in the dwarven underground who is visited by chefs and brewers from across all of Middle Earth. Even orcs and elves line up, wanting him to taste and evaluate their culinary creations. Sadly, Kridic dies of starvation in the end. While he spent his life tasting and judging the work of others, he forgot to really eat and digest any of it. He didn't let it in.

In my early Christianity, I was Kridic—and I ended up with an empty hole inside of me as a result. I was spiritually starving while filling the inner void with fattening counterfeits, blind to my own vice—looking to the speck in my brother's eye only to realize that it was the back of the log in my own. I thought it appeared virtuous to deflect a compliment when, in reality, all I was doing was refusing to receive the gift of gratitude from my neighbor. In a masquerade of righteousness, such deflection was actually egotistical. I'd become the unknowing product of an overly critical culture, acting as though I had everything to offer but nothing to receive. Thankfully, God wrote straight with my crooked lines; when I put my foot in my mouth, heckling that keynote speaker, He used the experience to show me myself.

DISCUSSION

Criticism Taken Too Far

My deficiency of reception was undoubtedly a manifestation of sinful pride; I'd go so far as to call it the chief symptom. In looking at the world around me, I see that I'm not alone in this vice. In a fault-finding pandemic of self-importance that has infected humanity since her exile from Eden, we have all tasted the dysfunction of narcissism at least to some extent. Of course, constructive feedback and tough discipline have their proper place; in fact, true love demands them. I would never claim otherwise. Yet, criticism has gotten entirely out of hand in our day, at the deadly expense of reception. I think any honest soul can admit that we sometimes struggle to humbly receive from God and neighbor, to lower ourselves, to really *let in* what others have for us.

Today's culture has trained us to perceive the world as being presented to us for our appraisal, rather than something to be received for our own benefit. For instance, YouTube videos include the classic "thumbs up" or "thumbs down" options, offering everybody the chance to grade what they saw on a pass/fail scale. Personally, I feel disheartened when, after enjoying some gorgeous performance by a church choir on YouTube, I see that 117 people out there wanted to make sure the choir knew that they gave the performance a "thumbs down." How about just watching something else if you don't like it? The appropriate response to a gift is "Thank you."

Other examples of struggling to receive abound. Notice the number of hit television shows based more upon analyzing performers than delighting in the performances themselves. Notice how many sporting events center more upon judging the athletes than upon enjoying the game itself. We can hardly leave a movie or a restaurant without hearing a plethora of unsolicited critique down to the details of an actor's wardrobe or a server's complexion. We're missing out on one another. The situation is tragic.

Love Doesn't Just Give; Love Also Receives

As we will see throughout this whole healing expedition, love is central. It's central because love is definitive of God and, therefore, definitive of the human race that God created in His image. I would thus define *healing* as God's *repairing of charity* within broken people — the restoration of our true selves as human reflections of divine love. One of the areas in which the love within us has been most fractured by sin — one of the foundational areas where we need healing the most — regards humble reception. In our sinful pride, we prefer to be the ones doing the giving. We're not as comfortable *letting in* the input of others.

In truth, love is never merely giving; rather, real love both gives and receives. First, and of course, love gives. Self-donation is a central component to love, best demonstrated by Christ "who, though he was in the form of God, did not count equality with God a thing to be grasped, but emptied himself, taking the form of a servant, being born in the likeness of men. And being found in human form he humbled himself and became obedient unto death, even death on a cross" (Phil. 2:6–8). Giving of ourselves in self-donation is clearly a vital part of godly love.

Christ Demonstrates Humble Reception

At the same time, the love of Christ was not limited to self-sacrifice alone; He also exemplified reception. Jesus received healthy input from others, such as the suggestion that He should come to the aid of Lazarus (John 11:1–11). Likewise, He received His Blessed Mother's request to perform the wedding miracle in Cana, which would identify Him as God's Anointed One and launch His public ministry (John 2:3–8). He also received Peter's repentance after the chief apostle had betrayed Him (John 21:15–19). He received Zacchaeus' hospitality (Luke 19:1–10) and the assistance of Simon of Cyrene (Luke 23:26). Other examples abound, such as His reception of Martha's service and Mary's attention (Luke 10:38–42), or the time that He allowed His feet to be washed (Luke 7:37–38). And, He repeatedly and earnestly requested the company and the prayers of His friends (Mark 14:32–42).

We find from all of these examples that Jesus' love was never limited to outpouring alone, but always accompanied by a welcomed inpouring of love from others. He didn't position Himself as *always the one doing the giving*. He didn't miss love's reception piece, and neither can we. Pope Benedict XVI makes this truth explicit when he says that "man cannot live by oblative, descending love alone. He cannot always give, he must also receive."[2]

Spiritual Asthma

By analogy, we might liken the giving and receiving sides of love to natural breathing. The giving side of love is the exhale — it's what our hearts put out there for others. The receiving side of love is the inhale — it's what we let in. Mature love is like healthy respiration in which we both give and receive, both exhale and inhale. If we posture ourselves toward the world around us as always giving, never receiving, then it's as though we suffer from spiritual asthma. As we know from asthma, if you're not inhaling properly, then you're not exhaling properly either.

Mother of the Virtues

For me, the key that unlocked lasting weight loss was mature receiving. Why is this receiving side of love so essential? In short, humility is a prerequisite for all healing. Before anything else, we have to stop playing God and humbly receive from our Creator and from our neighbor in order to grow.

As Augustine says, "If you ask me what is the first thing in religion, I will reply that the first, second, and third thing is humility."[3] Before I could embrace the virtue of self-care, I needed to learn how to receive—period. That is, self-care wouldn't cure gluttony until humility cured at least some of my pride. Taking better care of myself would never have entered the picture if I couldn't receive the truth about my need to lose weight, if I couldn't welcome the love of others who stood by me through the process, or couldn't accept the grace of God that makes redemption possible. In other words, a humble heart is required. As Mother Teresa says, humility is the "mother of all virtues."[4] Self-care is humility's offspring.

The Difficulties of Humility

Receiving can be difficult because it requires childlike vulnerability. We must let go of our hoisted posture that affords us with the illusion of control and, instead, be vulnerable to letting in that which God has prepared for us through our neighbor. Receiving from others can also be difficult because of our imperfections. In our sinful state, dysfunction accompanies our gifts of self. In turn, the faults that we all still possess can easily steal our focus away from God's image in one another. But, as my mom used to say, "Can we digest the meat and spit out the bones, rather than focusing on the bones to the point of choking on them—and missing out on the meat?"

The Fruits of Humility

The difficulties notwithstanding, learning to humbly receive was a revelation that changed everything for me. It was the most wonderful sort of transformation! Whenever I attended conferences, I no longer postured myself toward the presenters as their performance reviewer. Instead, I was hungry and excited for the feast that God wanted to give me through them. Attending such events wasn't miserable anymore; they were fun. At Mass, I was no longer a theological analyst looking for accidental heresies in the homily. Instead, I realized that I was a work in progress, in desperate need of the liturgies of both Word and Sacrament, filled with gratitude that I got to participate for one glorious hour in the activity of Heaven itself.

When reading theology, my primary question changed from "where did the writer miss the mark?" to "what does God have for me through this blessing?" — and the change brought peace. Watching movies became more enjoyable than when I had fancied myself a film critic. The deflection of compliments in a spirit of false humility gave way to reception and joy — by recognizing that all glory belongs to God.

And, whenever I encountered the inevitable "bones" of error from other works in progress like myself, I remembered that the Church is a hospital for the sick; I, too, was diagnosed with the terminal cancer of sin, and I, too, was in the care of the Great Physician, the only One who could heal me. The bones were no longer my focus, and I was no longer starving. My ongoing realization that "it's not all about me" and the corresponding reception of love from others brought life — as healthy respiration tends to do.

With regard to gluttony, humility began the healing process. Specifically, by learning to humbly receive, I came to recognize that I was in fact obese. Humility showed me a truthful, accurate picture of myself: although I wasn't essentially a problem, I certainly *had* a problem — a deeply ingrained sin that was robbing me blind of my fullest happiness. In humility, I recognized that obesity affected my relationships with God, self, and others. I realized that overeating was an instance of self-harm, an attack against God's beautiful image within me. And, it didn't just hurt me. It hurt those who cared about me and restricted what I had to offer them. For their sake and my own, taking better care of my body became *worth it*; after all, it is not problem-solving but *love* that ultimately moves us. Finally, through humility, I could receive the grace that heals me. The cultivation of a humble, receptive heart has been — in all of these ways — a much happier way to live!

APPLYING THE CONCEPTS ACROSS THE BOARD

In whatever areas you long for wellbeing, you simply cannot go wrong grounding your entire healing process on the foundation of humility. Whatever stands in the way of your fullest happiness, it's no match for the sovereign King before whom every knee will bow (Phil. 2:10–11). Anxiety, trauma, addiction, depression, disorder, and dysfunction — the Great Physician knows precisely what is needed for each and every problem and how to administer that grace.

Different conditions will involve their own specifics, of course, but, in every case, the Lord has the cure. In every case, the Lord *is* the cure. Thus, whenever we humble ourselves before God to receive His grace, mercy, love, and company, we have opened ourselves up to the path of life. In our pride, we all have the bad habit of telling God how big the storm is. In humility, we get to tell the storm how big our God is.

Tuning into the Counselor

Getting Practical

AT THIS POINT in my journey, the unity of reality had already shown me a couple of key ingredients to a more complete approach to healing. I realized that the healing process is based upon God, not the sin. I also saw my dire need for humility—and that I'd be going nowhere without it. Such realizations are wonderful; however, it's not enough just to recognize that these things are true. I needed to act. In fact, these awakenings themselves had indicated the need for action. To ground the healing process upon God is to center our healing upon love, since God is love. And love is, as the song by the band Boston describes, "more than a feeling."[1] What are the hands-on steps that will make the healing of Love's image within us concrete? The first practical measure is one whose importance is impossible to overstate. I'm talking about prayer.

A Peculiar Request

During my ministry as a Baptist pastor, while my weight was still at its heaviest, I received a phone call from the local sheriff during the middle of the night—a call that would take my prayer life to an unprecedented level. When I answered the phone, the sheriff introduced himself, and then he asked me to meet him at 4 a.m. on the side of the road. Feeling both curious and concerned, I accepted his invitation and drove to the specified location. Still under the dark of night, I spotted his parked car, pulled up behind it, got out of my vehicle, and walked over to where he was standing.

He started, "I'm sorry for the obscure time and place, but I can't risk anyone seeing us. Do you know that girl, Jackie, in your youth group? She's sixteen years old, and she has a little sister in the children's ministry?"

"Yes, Jackie's great! She's one of our most involved youths."

"Pastor, she's living in a house that's running drugs. Serious drugs, like cocaine. I know it. I've been working on this bust for a long time. I'll get straight to the point. I need you to schedule an afternoon house visit with them at some point soon. You get in there, under the guise of *pastor*—or do whatever you need to do—but you find out where they're hiding the drugs. Then you call me! Now, after the arrest, there is a possibility that the sisters could be separated by the foster care system, but at least they will be out of there. You want to help those children, and I want my bust. This is a win-win."

I asked the officer, "Have you tried someone else for this?"

He answered, "Yeah, I got one of Jackie's friends. And that girl actually found the drugs. But unfortunately, they had noticed her snooping around. By the time I showed up, they'd already moved the drugs."

The Truth Confirmed

Later that week, I went to that same friend of Jackie's and asked her, "Is this all true?"

"Oh yeah. The sheriff sent me in, all right. And I *did* find the coke, and I called him—but they hid it somewhere else before he showed up."

Afterward, I talked to Jackie, and she confirmed everything, too. She said, "I know what my parents are doing, the sheriff's right.

But I don't want them splitting up me and my sister. You can't let them do that to us. I'm all she's got. That's why I won't come forward. As long as that's possible, I'm keeping my mouth shut. And I don't want you to do that to me—don't you get us split up!"

A Moral Conundrum

I found myself facing a dilemma. I could either misrepresent my identity as a pastor while working as an undercover deputy on the sheriff's authority—and risk separating these two sisters—or I could refuse to do as he requested and risk their wellbeing as they would continue to be raised in an unhealthy and dangerous environment.

I was in one of those ethical conundrums where you're damned if you do, and you're damned if you don't. It seemed to be a no-win scenario—the kind that ethicists love to study. But, with Jesus Christ, there is no such thing as a no-win scenario. I invited the Holy Spirit into the situation, actively soliciting His guidance in radical dependency. Taking my prayer life to a new level of intensity and connection, I asked the Lord what to do. *He answered.*

God Answers Prayer

I didn't have to misrepresent myself, sneaking around Jackie's house hunting for a stash of narcotics. I didn't have to risk splitting up the sisters. And, I didn't have to knowingly let two children remain in a house of drug trafficking, either. When I silenced myself in prayer and really *listened* to the other end of the conversation, God provided an answer. It wasn't audible; it was clearer than that. The Lord prompted me, "Have Jackie sing at church." The message was clear as a bell.

I chose a song for Jackie to sing at one of our services, and she came regularly to the church to practice, bringing her little sister and a woman from the congregation with her. For the time being,

I was thankful that we got those girls out of the house—at least during the music practices.

On the day of Jackie's performance, her parents were so excited about their little girl's singing debut that they came to church for the first time. Hearing their daughter sing to Jesus moved them, and they responded to the altar call at the close of that morning's service. Afterward, members of the local community lovingly confronted them about what, apparently, many people knew was going on.

Jackie's parents converted to Christianity, then also came forward to the authorities and confessed everything. The family worked it out to have Jackie and her little sister raised by their grandparents. By God's miraculous design, the parents faced responsibility. The kids stayed together. They were now in a stable and loving home, not in the foster care system. And, Jackie's parents now know Jesus.

There is nothing in academic methodology for this. There is no formula for this. You're not going to find a line in the DSM–5 that says, "Have Jackie sing at church." Whenever options A and B are both no good, there *is* an unseen option C—but it's not something that we can discover in our own rubrics. We thus come to a fact as convicting as it is comforting: we aren't the ones in control. God is there for us. When we invite Him in, into our daily lives, He gets involved *because He cares about us* (1 Pet. 5:7).

A Deepened Prayer Life Results

It's no coincidence that my healing from obesity began soon after this powerful display of the Holy Spirit's guidance and saving grace in Jackie's family. It's not that I had no prayer life before; in fact, my journey out of agnosticism and into Baptist ministry had witnessed some undeniably powerful prayer experiences. Rather, God's work in Jackie's family took the Lord's daily guidance that we receive in prayer and made it real to me at a deeper level.

As a result of this landmark experience, I began seeking the Lord's guidance much more intentionally than before. I sought it specifically with regard to losing weight. In my conscience, I began hearing "you don't need to eat that" as clearly as I'd heard "have Jackie sing at church." As it turns out, the most important practical step to weight loss was neither portion control nor exercise. Rather, the victory started with prayer.

DISCUSSION

The Primacy of Prayer

Occasionally, we've all heard ourselves say, "At this point, *all we can do is pray*," as though prayer constitutes some high-risk, last-minute resort that probably won't work. Which came first, the ridiculous diminishment of prayer, or referring to a last-ditch-effort football pass as a "Hail Mary"? To reduce prayer in this way is like saying, "At this point, all we can do is ask our benevolent and independently wealthy Dad—who already offered to share His fortune with us—for a couple bucks."

Saying Prayers versus Praying

The Bible tells us to *pray constantly* (1 Thess. 5:17). This directive is not a hyperbole—an intentional exaggeration for effect. We can and should, in fact, pray without stopping. How can we do this, in light of all our other responsibilities? To answer this question, notice that the Bible does not say that we should "say prayers constantly." *Reciting prayers* is not the same thing as *prayer*. Saying prayers can be part of prayer. It can also be a great way to start praying. Yet, saying prayers can also interfere with prayer. If so, we should stop our recitation and start praying.[2]

True Prayer as Tuning into God

Prayer, in its fullest sense, is a state of communion with God in which the two-way communication lines remain open. It's an ongoing receptivity to the Holy Spirit's perpetual guidance, promptings, and care. Personally, I compare prayer to the process of tuning out the wrong radio frequencies so that I can tune into God's perpetual broadcast.[3] It's as though we're choosing the radio station that we'll have playing throughout all our daily activities.

Saying recitative prayers helps us to tune in, and it definitely starts the process. Saying prayers is indeed a big part of prayer. Yet, even after we finish *saying prayers*, prayer itself can continue. This can happen when we're listening, receiving, adoring the Lord, filled with wonder, worship, and gratitude, and attentive to His communications in our consciences. We can enjoy His company. Or, perhaps, on any given day, we might be angry with Him; nonetheless, we're in communion with Him. Prayer is a communication link. It's a relational bond. It's a state of union.

How We Can Pray

In particular, we can start the process by reciting any number of our favorites. The prayer of St. Francis, David's psalms, the Our Father, and quotes throughout the *Confessions* of St. Augustine — the whole book of which is one massive prayer — there are so many great ones. The Hail Mary is excellent, too, and I don't mean desperate football passes. By reciting these prayers, a person can slowly remove the obstacles that would otherwise clutter "the branch's link to the vine" (see John 15:5). Indeed, saying prayers can assist us in reaching that desired state of ongoing receptivity to God's perpetual communication. They help us *tune in*.

After a connection is made, we might then take some time to actively listen to what our Lord is broadcasting. We hear that we are beloved, individually-crafted reflections of the beautiful Creator, who made us to love Him and to be loved by Him. We remember that we are made to be God's covenant partner, His bride, friend, brother, child, and temple of His Spirit. We remember that Jesus died for each one of us. When we pray, the agony that we feel over our sin meets the divine mercy of God. We hear again that God takes delight in us, and the connection unescapably moves us to love.

The bond then becomes an unobstructed avenue for us to re-ceive — throughout the remainder of the day — the Lord's mercy, guidance, counsel, assistance, promptings, gifts, conviction, and company. Grafted into God through this intimate communication link, the branch can now receive the life that the vine supplies. Tun-ing out the frenzied inputs of fear and strife that want to come from Satan, a fallen world, and our own sin is a lovely experience in and of itself! Surpassing the pleasant quieting of this world's noise, God's broadcast is a symphony — you haven't lived until you've heard that.

Prayer: Don't Try Healing without It

As communal as prayer is in the universal body of Christ, it also has a very personal element to it. In whatever ways you best tune into the Lord, *do that first*, before proceeding into any subsequent phase of the healing process. As healing is all grace, don't try to do it on your own. Or, if you learn the way I did, you can try going it alone. Bookmark this page; then, after realizing that trying to heal by your own power is a joke, return to this spot and keep reading. You'll receive no judgment from me; I learned about the necessity of prayer the hard way.

The Holy Spirit's Daily Guidance Is Like the Wind

When it comes to healing, prayer — like humility — is foundational and nonnegotiable. But it can be a challenge. Although the Lord is available to us as our Advocate, Helper, or Counselor (John 14:16, 26; 16:7), we sometimes struggle, or even forget, to talk to Him. For me, difficulties with prayer regard the Holy Spirit being "like the wind" (John 3:8; 20:22; Ezek. 37:9–14; Acts 2:2). We cannot see the wind or pick it up and show it to somebody. How, then, do we communicate with someone unseen?

Understandably, it can be a challenge to talk to somebody we can't see. At the same time, however, notice that nobody doubts the wind's real existence—especially if they've survived a tornado or a hurricane. Even though we can't see it, nobody relegates the wind to some ethereal, distant, or magical notion. We know it's real. We know it's real because we experience its *movement*. Like the wind, the Holy Spirit is literally real, and we can sense His movements directing us. When we pray, we hoist our sails.

Through prayer, we can finally invite the Lord into whatever issues are weighing us down. When we tune in, hoisting our sails to catch the wind's direction, we will sense the Lord moving us away from harm and toward real life. On our own, we can't see the fatal undertows or sharks lurking beneath the relaxed, glassy surface of our comfort zones. But, through prayer, the Lord shows us these dangers. He shows us that the deadliest waters are often the ones that appear calm, serene, and comfortable—such as eating whatever we feel like eating, doing whatever we've always done, turning to quick-fixes, or just not thinking about it. God also reveals that the rough, uncomfortable waters of change mark the way forward—in my case, changes such as eating well and exercising. In our weaknesses, His power can be made perfect as we come to know that we are not alone. Through His guidance, we will know that He is with us, wants the best for us, and will help us.

APPLYING THE CONCEPTS
ACROSS THE BOARD

The Lord really is more watchfully involved in our day-to-day affairs than we can possibly imagine. He is closely engaged in *your* daily life. In all of your needs for healing, no matter what they may be, He sees you. In every smile, in every moment tinged with sorrow, and in every emotion that no words can aptly describe, He is there.

> It's not just that He lives in our soul like a tabernacle—although that's a good image—but it's rather that He occupies our whole being! This can be understood very realistically, not metaphorically. The Lord says, "I am the vine; you are the branches" (John 15:5). Just as the life that is in the vine surges through the branches ... the very Life of Jesus Christ surges through us. The Spirit living within us is sometimes called the Divine Artist because He is actively transforming us.[4]

The Lord is truly there with you, right now, as present as a person who is literally sitting in the next chair. His guidance and assistance are real. Whatever the area of need, invite Him into your healing process; the Divine Artist wants to make you His next work of art. Quiet your weary and cluttered heart, tune out the wrong frequencies, and hear from your Lord that He is a Great Physician, and He is *right there*.

SEVEN

Engaging Body, Mind, and Soul

The New Foundation

I HAD FIRST seen the scale read 303 pounds while I was working in Texas as a full time Baptist pastor, pursuing my Master's degree in Theology, and teaching on the side. It was during the following twelve months that I took my initial baby steps in centering the healing process upon God rather than problem-solving—although I didn't fully appreciate this idea nor the language for it until much later. It was also within this same year that I experienced the graduate colloquium that God had used to convict me of my need for humility. The events surrounding Jackie's family, which God had used to deepen my prayer life, happened during this season as well. Interestingly, it all coincided with my enrollment in RCIA and my entry into the Catholic Church.

In other words, this important year of my life introduced me to the healing concepts that, together, laid the correct foundation for lasting healing: God's sovereignty over the problem, the importance of humbly receiving from others, and a deepened reliance upon the daily guidance of the Holy Spirit through prayer. Granted, I was still immersed in weight-loss gimmicks during this period, but the journey toward victory was finally underway. And, my understanding of each of these lessons would deepen with time.

Throughout my first few years as a Catholic, as all of these foundational truths sank deeper, I still seesawed back and forth between weight loss and weight gain—but, gradually, the scale reading went down. I finally stopped returning to the dreadful 300-pound mark, and I continued to witness the transforming power of sacramental grace.

A few years after my conversion, the new recipe for healing had resulted in the first "half century" of *lasting* fat loss, having gotten my bodyweight down to 250 pounds without bouncing back. At this point in my life, I left behind all the weight-loss gimmicks that had previously made me feel like a problem to be fixed. Instead, I simply asked God in daily prayer for the grace to take better care of myself through basic portion control and exercise. On the one hand, my weight never climbed above 250 again. On the other hand, it stopped dropping.

Becoming Catholic as the Beginning of the Story

My first several years as a Catholic thus drove home a twofold message. The first was that an intensified embrace of God's sovereignty, the virtue of humility, and a rich prayer life did indeed lay a powerful basis for personal healing. The second was that this groundwork by itself would only take me so far. After all, becoming Catholic isn't the end of the story—it's the beginning.[1] God had other graces for me to build upon this foundation; but whatever those measures were, they still eluded me. After losing the first fifty without backlash, my progress froze as I hit "the plateau from hell." I would stay there for more than ten years.

But, even with this plateau, the physical factors of my healing—eating right and working out—were now connected to the undergirding spiritual factors of God's sovereignty, my need for humility, and the necessity of prayer. In short, my new foundation for healing recognized that I'm more than just a functioning pile of cells. Rather, I am a union of body and soul. I'd tasted my first sustainable results because I was finally attending to both.

DISCUSSION

The Union of Body and Soul

Our Trinitarian Creator is a divine union of Father, Son, and Spirit—multiple Persons that are one God. In a sense, God is a complex unity. Correspondingly, the people He made in His image are a complex unity—multiple things that are one thing. To be clear, the finite human is one person, unlike the infinite Creator, who is three Persons. Nevertheless, mirroring the complexity of our Maker, we are a multiplicity of different domains that are all one human being. We have bodily domains and spiritual domains that are interconnected and occur together as a unified whole—a "complex body-soul unity."[2]

Our Bodily Domain

It's helpful to clarify the different parts of our complexity so that we can better understand how they interact across the process of our healing. First, we have a bodily domain that includes the five senses, basic cognitive powers, and natural emotions.[3] In God's incredible design, the body allows us to access the data of reality with our senses, and then it cognitively processes this data into a meaningful picture—rather than a random jumble of inputs. Better yet, through physiological drives and embodied emotions, we can even respond to reality. What this means is that feelings of hunger, pleasure, "fight or flight," attraction, sadness, and happiness can all further enable us to interact with the world around us in meaningful ways.[4]

Our Spiritual Domain

The human soul has its own abilities. One of these is the power of higher reasoning—which, incidentally, is also proof that we have a soul.[5] Surpassing the limitations of the human brain, we're aware *that we're aware*, and that we can ponder the mysteries of our being. This ability, also called *rationality* or *consciousness*,[6] is truly astounding. As Pascal marveled, the person is like a "feeble reed" blowing around on the vast ocean of the universe; yet, the tiny reed is self-aware of this, something that sets its value uniquely apart and above any infinite void of time and space.[7]

What a power we have in reason, especially when it partners with faith! In these instances, we can take flight toward the mysterious fullness of our purpose.[8] And, if we let it, the wonder of human rationality can fill us with sheer awe at our Creator's majesty. At the same time, there is a danger for us to remain mindful of when it comes to reasoning about reason. In particular, this capacity is so extraordinary that we can be tempted to totalize it to the neglect of everything else.[9] We cannot forget the role of our senses, feelings, and choices. Nor can we forget that sin brings disorder to each part of us, or that each part of us needs Christ's healing.

The spiritual part of the human being also includes free will. Free will, or *volition*, regards our ability to make decisions that may differ from bodily appetites, natural instincts, and reflexive impulses. Against the force of strong bodily drives, our free will enables us to rise above physical instincts, even to the nobility of self-sacrifice. This God-given spiritual power, like higher reason, renders us capable of self-transcendence.

Also indicative of our spiritual domain are yearnings that transcend bodily reflex. Beyond the basic emotions of anger, fear, and happiness, we also experience the deepest of longings, passions, joys, and sorrows. We have a "God-shaped hole"[10] that cries out to be filled, a part of us that knows we're meant to be loved in a supernatural way, a homesickness for a place we've never seen, and a secret chamber within which — if we listen — we can hear our Lord calling to us. These more profound experiences arise from within the human soul, referred to by some people as *ensouled emotion.*[11] Higher reason, free will, and our deepest yearnings are all indicative of the human soul. They all show that there is more to us, the beings whom God created in His own image, than merely physical bodies.

Clarifying the Language: The Union of Body and Soul

Finally, we must note that our bodily and spiritual domains occur *in union* with each other. They are not separate. Rather, all of these component parts are inherently interlaced with one another—they happen together. Sensory perception, basic cognition, and embodied emotions all engage the soul in their expression. At the same time, higher reasoning, free will, and ensouled emotions all engage the body in their expression.[12] While we can say accurately that some of our abilities come mainly from the body and others mainly from the soul, they're all connected in an inseparable way.[13] Perhaps the union of body and soul is best seen in our remarkable ability to form interpersonal bonds of friendship that grow stronger over time. After all, relationships engage our senses, feelings, thoughts, choices, and deepest longings, all at the same time.

How Body and Soul Interact with Each Other

Practically speaking, the secret to the interior wholeness that therapeutic self-help books seek rests in our bodily and spiritual components operating in agreement.[14] Whenever body and soul battle disorder, they can actually seem as though they're at odds with each other. But, where both align with God's will, we experience inner wholeness. Simply put, getting body and soul onto the same page—the *right* page—cultivates a wondrous sense of increasing completeness within us, as opposed to a worsening sense of internal fracture. How do we bring our physical side and our spiritual side into one accord? How do we get them onto the right page together? The lifelong journey begins with the interplay between them.

How the Soul Affects the Body

Recall that the human soul includes higher reasoning, free will, and our most profound longings. These spiritual parts of us certainly affect our bodies. Now, suppose you misuse your free will to choose a gluttonous binge. This exercise of your free will—an ability of the human soul—will have immediate and inevitable effects on your physical body. Specifically, your body becomes larger. Your blood pressure increases. Your energy levels decrease. Your body's tolerance increases such that it will take even more food and drink to produce the same endorphin release next time. In such an instance, your spiritual soul absolutely affects your physical body in negative ways that lead to frustration, depression, and regret—overall, a sense of inner rupture.

Conversely, imagine a positive example in which your soul's capacities for higher reasoning, free will, and the longing for ultimate goodness do lead you to make a healthy dinner. As a result, your body loses excess weight, your blood pressure drops, your energy levels increase, and the decision helps the bodily sensation of feeling full to recalibrate in a more balanced way. In this example, your spiritual soul absolutely affects your physical body in positive ways that lead to success, happiness, and gratitude—overall, a sense of inner wholeness. In both examples, notice how the soul affects the body.

How the Body Affects the Soul

Just as our spirituality affects our physicality, the reverse is also true: the body affects the soul. Suppose you feel particularly hungry one afternoon. This bodily appetite can influence your higher reasoning to rationalize a gluttonous splurge; it can tempt your free will to make the wrong decision; it can try to shout louder than your deeper longing for goodness; and it can further shape an erroneous conscience. In this example, your physical body absolutely affects your spiritual soul in negative ways that pull you in the wrong direction — resulting in an overall sense of inner conflict.

Now, imagine a positive example in which healthy eating habits have you accustomed to a balanced diet. Your eyes behold a buffet and hunger pangs kick in; however, the very thought of eating an excess of unhealthy, fattening foods actually turns your stomach. In fact, your bodily appetite craves a salad more than any other option on the buffet table. These healthy physical sensations, in turn, support your higher reasoning in discerning a good dinner decision, bolster your free will in making that decision, agree with your deeper longing for goodness, and lead to an increasingly clarified conscience. Simply put, since you already feel like doing the right thing, it makes it easier for you to discern and to make the right choice when confronted with a bad option — healthy bodily drives thus bring support to your spiritual capacities of reason and free will. In this example, your physical body absolutely affects your spiritual soul in positive ways that help propel you in the right direction — resulting in an overall sense of interior wholeness, as body and soul both align with God's plan for your happiness. In both examples, notice how the body affects the soul.

The Ongoing Interplay between the Physical and the Spiritual

In their union, the soul affects the body and the body affects the soul. We have here what is called a "reciprocal relationship" — or, *body-soul reciprocity*, if you want to really impress your friends. But the fancy language need not scare us. To say that body and soul occur in reciprocal relation to one another is simply to say that they each affect the other.[15] For better or worse, the soul affects the body, which affects the soul, which affects the body, which affects the soul, and so on, in an ongoing spiral.

APPLYING THE CONCEPTS ACROSS THE BOARD

An upward spiral, in which our physical domains and our spiritual ones mutually reinforce one another in the right direction, applies to every aspect of growth—and that is good news for every area of healing. For instance, the examples above can describe how a person is weaned off any unhealthy dependency, whether it be chemical, psychological, or both. From alcoholism to pornography addiction, every graced decision in the right direction both weakens an unhealthy dependence upon counterfeits and cultivates well-ordered avenues for true happiness. The healthier that reasoning and decision-making become, the more the body adapts; the more that the physical body adapts to health, the more support it brings to right reasoning and decision-making in the soul. Best of all, the more that body and soul heal in this way, the more whole we become.

Consider a man who seeks the healing of his ill temper. In the past, the bodily sensation of rage would prompt the man's soul to embrace bitterness and violence; whenever such hateful actions were chosen, it further fueled his rage, which further inclined his reason and will toward more violence, and so on. Eventually, the ill-tempered man became his own victim, torn apart by hatred. Internally fractured, he became his own worst enemy.

But, after turning to Christ for healing, the Lord reversed the downward spiral into an upward one. The next time the man felt enraged, he turned to God for help. With the assistance of grace, he reasoned in his spirit that vengeful actions would only bring more destruction to him and to his loved ones. Using his God-given spiritual ability to make decisions that differ from reflexive bodily emotions, he chose to stop his negative trajectory and to remove himself from the inflammatory situation until he calmed down. Temperance made him feel better, which encouraged more prayerful restraint in the future, which made him feel even better, and so forth.

Body-Soul Unity: A Summary

Created in the image of complexity, we are complex. That is, we exist as a mysterious union of the physical with the spiritual. Body-soul union is such an inherent part of us that we can't so much as choose to practice the guitar without our body developing corresponding finger callouses. The quest for inner wholeness requires that we attend to both parts of this complexity and to their interaction. Bodily strategies by themselves could never be enough.

In sum, a more complete and lasting approach to healing demands that we engage a larger picture of reality, one that honors human complexity by encompassing both the material and the transcendent. True wellbeing necessitates that we open ourselves up to the spiritual realities undergirding our condition. It requires that, in addition to physical measures, we employ the powers of the soul—appreciating that, in God's extraordinary design, the spiritual and physical parts of us each affect the other in their union. The healing path may be a messy and lifetime endeavor, but each tiny advance brings an increase in the abundant life meant for us. Every step along the way brings with it more inner wholeness than before, more resulting joy, more grace, and more life-changing glimpses into the heavenly destiny ahead.

PART III

VICE

FIGHTS

BACK

EIGHT

Vice's Assault Against Body-Soul Unity

Vice's Lingering Hold: Two Characteristic Tales

I COULD TELL endless stories about my seemingly eternal battle with the 250-pound plateau—but a couple of representative incidents will suffice. Each of these episodes took place around the three-year anniversary of my entry into the Church. During this period, much of my life looked considerably different than it had before. I was no longer living in Texas. I was back in Pittsburgh, close to where I had grown up. Overall, life was good: I worked on my Ph.D. in Theology at Duquesne University, and I taught a few courses on the side. Yet, amidst a host of fruitful changes, one not-so-good thing was the same—the plateau, which started to feel impossible to break.

Vice's Link to Disordered Feelings

In the first incident, I woke up one Monday morning feeling hopeful that the previous week of consistent diet and exercise may have at last moved the scale. Eagerly, I slid it out and stood on it, waiting to discover whether my recent work at the gym had paid dividends. Much to my dismay, the number 250 lit up yet again, in bright red. I stepped off the scale, and then I kicked it a smidgen too forcefully back into the corner, as though it were to blame.

Then, on Thursday evening, all my university friends suggested we should to go out to our favorite restaurant. When my eyes saw the picture of the bacon cheeseburger featured in the menu, the temptation—bolstered by the week-long caloric deficit and the frustrating scale reading—became unbearable. "I'll just go ahead and do it, before any pangs or conscience or holy decisions can stop me," I thought for a brief second. Then I ordered a shameful amount of food. I also drank more high-carb, inky beer than I care to admit—although it's worth mentioning that the beer was called "Skull Splitter" which, the following morning, lived up to its name. Soon afterward, the guilt kicked in. It feels similar to the experience of falling down, only the distinct plummeting sensation happens inside your spirit.

Weeks like the one I just described were all too common. Sometimes my motive for overeating was to fill a void that only mature love can fill. Other times I ate too much because I fell back into understanding myself essentially as a problem; then I treated myself according to how I saw myself—like garbage. Most times, I ate as a coping mechanism to escape from stress. Still other times, I just wanted to have some fun. Regardless of the specifics, all gluttonous splurges boiled down to a pivotal moment in which I said to myself, "I'll just go ahead and do it because I *feel* like it." In other words, the force of disordered emotions was apparently central to gluttony's grip.

Vice's Link to Disordered Reasoning

The second incident that I wish to share highlights the fact that disordered thinking was also in play. One particular Wednesday, a marathon schoolwork session kept me on campus late into the evening. Already past dinnertime, my appetite became distracting. I heard the "still small voice of the Lord" telling me that a healthy meal was all that was needed, and that His grace would be sufficient for me. Yet, instead of acquiescing to His lordship, I entered into a rationalizing dialogue with myself.

"I deserve a little fun after today," I thought to myself. "And imagine how much more clearly I'll think and how much more efficiently I'll work after this distracting hunger nuisance has been removed. I can binge just this once, without changing who I am." Then I went to an all-you-can-eat buffet where I proceeded to gorge myself.

I once heard somebody say that, by entering into a dialogue with our own self-justifying rationale, we're actually entering into a dialogue with the serpent. We know from the Garden of Eden how *that* goes. Indeed, this line of faulty reasoning described above has led me to many a buffet binge. In one such session of note, the restaurant cut me off. The server actually forbade me to return to the buffet. I complained, "But your buffet says, 'All you can eat.'" The server replied, "Right. That's *all you can eat!*"

In sum, I was face-to-face with the deadly sin of gluttony, and it is a terrible enemy. Vice drew its power over me from disordered feelings and disordered reasoning alike. My feelings would go from telling me that "overeating will make me feel better" to yelling at me for listening to them. Likewise, my mind would try to justify a splurge one moment, then a moment later call me *stupid* for thinking that way. Interestingly, gluttony always claimed that I could overeat without changing who I am. It was, in every case, a liar. It didn't make me feel better. It wasn't justified. And it most certainly changed me.

DISCUSSION

Fundamentally Good yet Disordered

To be clear, our emotional and reasoning abilities are gifts from God that are fundamentally good. When *well-ordered*, as God intended them to be, our feelings and thinking help propel us toward the life God wants for us. Yet, sin throws these God-given gifts into *disorder*, inclining us both emotionally and mentally toward that which would actually harm us.[1] In short, sin has a disordering, destructive, and irrational nature that turns us against ourselves.

Sin's Destructive Nature and the Tempter's Exploit

Sin, in its disordering agency, is a parasite. It saps our vitality. It survives within us by draining the life out of who we're supposed to be. While God's image in us cannot be totally destroyed by sin, certain aspects of His image can become warped — such as our God-given hunger for virtue, which sin diminishes.[2]

When we really take the Great Physician up on His offer to heal us and so begin to experience the concrete power of His grace in our lives, the sin within us doesn't die easily. Whenever it senses that its hold is starting to loosen and realizes that God's image is starting to clarify, sin tries to reassert its footing. It responds to God's healing power the same way that anything reacts when cornered by a more powerful rival who is about to destroy it — by screaming, clawing, and biting. Evil will fight for the perpetuation of its own parasitic existence.

Although our sinful dross was only ever a spiritual tumor, never a substantial part of our true selves made in God's image, when we die to it there is still a death—and it is natural to grieve in the face of death. In other words, our reasoning and emotions, in their irrational disorder, will sometimes "miss the sin" the way that we miss an old friend. The Bible vividly compares a freed person who backslides into former sin to a dog returning to his vomit (Prov. 26:11). Yet, there is a reason the dog goes back—and it is a tragic scene, indeed: we experience an emotional attachment to the vicious tendencies that imprison us, which incur in us a peculiar sense of endearment. We might call it "spiritual Stockholm syndrome."

Satan, of course, is right there to capitalize on these phenomena. We'd all prefer it if the devil graciously accepted defeat and bowed out quietly, but he actually does the opposite. Desperate to maintain the idols that keep us his slaves, he turns up the heat. He will suggest, tempt, and lie to us according to the gravity of our most harmful habits. In his arrogance and hatred, he will play on sin's destructive power. Make no mistake: we have a real enemy who seeks to unravel us.

You're Not Alone

If you find yourself missing sin like some prickly old security blanket that you got used to holding tight, know that everyone who follows Christ to salvation is right there with you. You are not alone. In fact, you find yourself in the company of the great saints of our Church—such as Augustine, who once prayed to the Lord, "Grant me chastity and continence, but not yet."[3] And if you find yourself strangely ingratiated to a harmful habit, tempted to backslide, or going through a grieving process over a slain vice—even though it used to hurt you—it's not because you are crazy. It's because *sin is crazy*, irrational by its nature. After all, what tempted the first humans to betray God was something that their heavenly Father had already provided in its proper form.

It is not just the other disciples of Christ who are with you; Christ Himself is with you as well. While He never sinned, He did enter the human condition, and He understands temptation firsthand. He knows you're going through it; He loves you, and He can relate. Some might think that Christ's perfection limits how much He can identify with us, but the opposite is true. In His perfect humanity, His capacity to empathize with us is perfect.

What's more, as the Great Physician, He knows perfectly what you need. He is right there with you to reinforce the truth: "I am your God, and I am jealous for you. You don't need the sin. What it claimed to provide was a lie. What it claimed to provide is something that I, the Bread of Life, will give to you in its fullness. Don't be afraid. Come with me, and *let me show you.*"

The Assault on Body-Soul Unity

At the center of vice's power to destroy is its *severing of body and soul.* The lies that vice whispers to both our heart and mind would have us believe that we can do whatever we want to our body without it having any effect on the soul. The opposite is true. As we explored in the previous chapter, God created us as a body-soul composite: they are connected in an inseparable way. Vice attacks this connection.

The Case of the Repentant Prostitute

One of my graduate professors told me an unforgettable story that made the importance of body-soul unity real to me in a pragmatic way. In particular, he told our class the story of his work as a Catholic counselor at a family therapy center where one of his clients was a prostitute.

She said to him, "I'm done with prostitution. I've quit, and I'll never go back."

He replied, "From our previous sessions together, you know I am *delighted* to hear this decision! Could you tell me a little bit about how you came to make this choice?"

"Prostitution made me miserable, unhappier than I ever thought possible," she answered. "You see, whenever I would see one of my 'clients' I would always say the same thing to him. I'd say, 'Do whatever you want to my *body*, but leave *me* out of it.'"

"And how did that make you feel?"

"It made me feel dead inside."

He responded, "It's no wonder it made you feel dead inside. You were treating your body as though it didn't make you present to the other person. We have a name for a body that no longer makes a soul present to other people. We call it a *corpse*. By saying, 'Do whatever you want to my *body*, but leave *me* out of it,' you treated your body like a corpse. That's why you felt dead."

The Sacramental Character of the Person

The testimony above illustrates well how sin attacks the union of body and soul. In turn, this idea of sin's assault upon body-soul unity helps us to better grasp why vice's retaliation is so fierce. To begin, the term "body-soul unity" is another way for us to describe our sacramental character as human beings. To explain, we cannot physically see or touch our spiritual souls. Yet, we can still encounter each other's souls. How? I encounter your soul by encountering the body that makes it truly present to me. We use this same language to describe the Eucharist: the consecrated Host truly "makes present" the Body, Blood, Soul, and Divinity of Christ.[4]

Building upon this insight, we can view all of creation through a sacramental lens, in which the physical is a conduit for the spiritual. Our sacramental worldview as Catholics recognizes that greater invisible realities (such as love and grace) are made present to us through the physical realities that we can access with our five senses (such as a natural wonder we see, a song we hear, or a human touch we feel). Our personhood possesses this wondrous sacramentality because our visible bodies make our invisible souls accessible to one another. When we encounter each other's bodies, we encounter each other's souls. To the point: when vice fights back, it targets our sacramental character. Playing on disordered feelings and disordered thinking alike, it works to rupture the union of body and soul—ripping us apart from the inside out.

APPLYING THE CONCEPTS ACROSS THE BOARD

While many of us haven't had to overcome a battle as intense as leaving behind a life of prostitution, we've all experienced a lost recognition of our body-soul unity at some point. We see it all the time in the virtual universe of the internet. In online interactions, from Twitter to email, it becomes easy for us to try to separate body from soul—doing and saying things that we would never say in a fully present, face-to-face encounter with another person. Online interactions are not wrong in and of themselves, yet they can be dangerous because they allow us to succumb to the deception that we're able to interact apart from our bodies. Surfing a virtual world while "leaving our bodies out of it" can have us do and say uncharitable things to one another, things that leave us feeling dead inside—having severed body from soul.

Vice can fracture our body-soul union through fornication, vicious web-trolling, and gluttony alike. Whether the example is prostitution, splitting virtual identities from real ones when surfing the web, or gluttony's false claim that we can abuse our bodies with no consequence to our integral personhood, each of these phenomena represents the same problem. Namely, they all attempt to separate our bodily aspects from our spiritual ones. They all treat our bodies like lifeless shells, as though they don't manifest our souls. In the end, all vice—because it attacks the image of God within us—is an assault upon our body-soul unity, to at least some degree. All sin works to disintegrate us.

We must remember, as we endeavor to hold our ground against vice's backlash, that God has created our bodies and souls to be temples of the Holy Spirit. The manner in which we treat this temple is no insignificant matter, and vice wages no insignificant assault against us. With God's grace, we can conquer plateaus and setbacks alike, but let's be honest about what we're up against — we're facing a formidable and retaliatory foe.

NINE

Ten Years Battling Emotions

Passions Personified

I'LL NEVER FORGET taking my niece, Sorsha, to Baskin-Robbins for ice cream back when she was a little girl. I asked, "What flavor are you going to pick? Baskin-Robbins has thirty-one different flavors of ice cream to choose from! Do you know which one you want?"

Sorsha replied, "Cookie-dough monkey ... chocolate-chip-mint monkey ... *fight!*"

Then she simply sat there in her car seat. She remained silent for a moment, making no movements, except for her eyes, which were darting back and forth with mental intensity. No additional context was provided, yet none was needed. I knew exactly what she was talking about—and I could picture the scene vibrantly.

I imagined her appetite for cookie-dough ice cream personified as this interior monkey warrior, armed with a glinting breastplate and determined to win his desired territory. Meanwhile, her appetite for chocolate-chip-mint ice cream was also wearing polished armor and carrying his monkey spear, equally resolute to capture the terrain of Sorsha's free will. Then I envisioned these two gladiators doing glorious battle against each other—like Hector and Achilles of old. Yet all I actually saw was the continual jerking motion of my niece's eyes, as though an android from Star Trek was processing an overload of data.

Eventually, the eye movements ceased, and she smiled and breathed a sigh of relief. She looked back at me and said, "Chocolate-chip-mint monkey wins."

Now *my* eyes darted back and forth, as my own head was swimming with the anointed insight that comes only from the mind of a child. My wee niece had just given me simple, accessible language for describing the same interior war that St. Paul wrestles with in his lofty compositions. That is, whenever I struggle with my bodily drives, it's as though I'm struggling with inner monkeys. My passions, my fleshly appetites, my emotions — they could all be personified in this way. From that day on, Sorsha's metaphor was common language throughout all the Murphy households: we would regularly refer to sleepy monkey, hungry monkey, angry monkey, good-mood monkey, and so forth whenever we wanted an accessible way to talk about our feelings and desires.

The Ten-Year Plateau

Lacking the proper way to understand and respond to these inner monkeys, my healing process hit its temporary ceiling. The characteristic battles against vice described in the previous chapter lingered throughout this entire period, repeating themselves over and over again like an old, scratched, vinyl record that keeps skipping backward.

I eventually found myself looking back at ten years on the same plateau, wondering if I would ever be free. At this point in my life, I had completed my Ph.D., had been married for a few years, moved to South Carolina, and was now teaching several courses remotely for Divine Mercy University. God had been forming me in a number of different areas, but gluttony's defeat still eluded me. While the grace of God had me prospering in my marriage and my career, I still weighed exactly 250 pounds.

By now, I was at least intellectually aware that splurges were as harmful as they were unsatisfying; I knew that I needed to advance in self-care in order to thrive in my humanity more authentically—more reflective of the image that truly defines me. That is, I realized in my head that virtue makes us happy and accurate, whereas vice makes us sad and dumb. Yet, what made sense in my head still felt light years away from connecting to my heart. How often St. Paul's words echo in my own conscience: "For I do not do the good I want, but the evil I do not want is what I do" (Rom. 7:19).

Blaming Emotions

I've heard it said that the distance between head and heart is massive. I liken it to the people of God wandering for forty years in the wilderness. It's not that the Promised Land was geographically far away. But it takes decades to get anywhere when you keep going in circles.

> Like a man in a carriage endlessly circling an urban round-about, those suffering from anxiety and depression find themselves trapped in a circular rut of distorted logic. The problem is the reasoning embedded in distorted passions. ... What the anxious or depressed person needs, in short, is to get off the psychological bus whose destination is nowhere, that is, to perform what Chesterton calls the "voluntary, vigorous, and mystical act" of getting out at Gower Street. ... [The] "mystical act" of stepping out of the circular rut.[1]

My own roundabout rut of distorted logic revolved around a fundamentally negative perception of my emotions.

Because they often caused me grief in their disorder, I viewed my emotions as "the bad guy," and then exhausted my energy trying to fight them. I wasn't actually fighting sin. I was fighting myself. Each battle would inevitably tire me out, leaving me vulnerable again to vice's lingering stronghold. If I was ever going to get off the ten-year plateau, then I would have to exit this go-nowhere circle. In particular, I needed to recognize my emotions, passions, and appetites as reflective of God's image within me and appreciate my feelings as the God-given part of me that they are. Until I did, I'd continue to reduce myself to a problem, fight myself, and remain stuck.

DISCUSSION

Emotions as Part of God's Image

When disordered, it can be easy for us to oversimplify emotion as "bad"—especially after our feelings and appetites get us into trouble. Yet, this does not have to be the case. *Every* part of our body-soul union reflects the image of God, including our capacity for feeling.

God Is Emotional

Could you even imagine God without emotion? Jesus revealed the heavenly Father as the "Abba" (Daddy) of the prodigal son, who leaps off the porch to embrace his wayward boy upon returning home, and then throws a grand celebration (Luke 15:11–32). Look at the emotion in that scene! Or imagine what each Divine Person of the Holy Trinity felt when the anguished Son prayed in earnest for His Father to "remove this cup," as "his sweat became like great drops of blood falling down upon the ground" (Luke 22:42–44). We repeatedly witness God experiencing a whole range of emotion through His embodiment in the Incarnation, as Jesus felt distressed (Matt. 26:37), amazed (Luke 7:9), angry (Mark 3:5), happy (Luke 10:21), stressed out (Luke 22:44), peaceful (John 14:27), and sad (John 11:35). Crafted after God's own likeness, we are also profoundly emotional.

Emotions are Not the Bad Guy

Realizing that we're not fundamentally problems to be solved means realizing that emotions themselves are not problems but a beautiful part of God's image within us. As one scholar explains,

Our passions and desires are like the steeds, to use Plato's legendary metaphor, which, while needing to run and unruly, are the 'erotic' drive that propels us on toward the highest Beauty and the highest Good.[2]

In other words, our passions, bodily drives, appetites, and feelings—our inner monkeys—are an important part of us that reflects God's image, designed to both express and to direct us further toward true love.

God wired into us a deep inclination to well-ordered emotions, directed toward all that is good, true, and beautiful. Thanks to emotions, we can encounter the sweetest affections within otherwise purely mundane toil. Through feelings, we experience hope amidst our sacrifice. Our emotions liven the otherwise mechanical activities of survival with a profound sense of purpose. They animate our relationships with a vitality that surpasses mere stimulus and response. Our feelings drive us with the desire for *more*—more development, more healing, more wholeness. And, through emotion, we experience a palpable attraction to God's call for us to live out our humanity as He intended.[3]

Our Need for Emotion

We need emotions; in truth, our wellbeing depends upon them. Our God-given reason, as crucial as it is, is not enough by itself for us to live rightly. We can all remember times when our thinking processes became rigid, cold, or unsympathetic—such as times when we fell into the sin of gossip. Our statements may very well have been technically accurate during such occasions, but we lost what matters most. St. Paul warns us that, in the absence of love, even if we fathomed all knowledge, we'd amount to nothing more than noise-makers (1 Cor. 13:1).

It is when our thinking processes are the most disordered that our feelings come to the rescue. The joyful emotions that accompany gratitude will break down the defensive walls we sometimes build in our friendships. The warmth of compassionate affection will melt the ice of indifference. And by sharing in the sorrow and happiness of others, our feelings will eradicate the heart-callous of taking one another for granted. In these ways, emotions are God's instrument to "remove from your body the heart of stone and give you a heart of flesh" (Ezek. 36:26). Though I would never totalize the phrase "follow your heart," there are certainly times when we should.

The Good beneath the Disordered Manifestations of Emotions

When it comes to disordered emotions, all unhealthy yearnings have some natural-law-good underneath them that God emblazoned into our being. That is, when God created us, He wrote His way of love into our hearts.[4] These desires that God imprinted within us can certainly misfire in disordered ways through sin, but the disordered manifestation itself is the problem — not the root desires within us. For instance, beneath lust is the God-given passion for romance, which itself is good and comes from God's love for us and our origin as relational persons. Beneath vicious laziness is the desire for Sabbath rest. Beneath rage is a sense of injustice which, when warranted, is the heart of valid anger. And, beneath inordinate food cravings, there is a healthy yearning for the goods of creation, an appetite that protects life.

The Example of St. Paul

By way of example, think about St. Paul's emotional intensity — the man used to *hunt people* for a living. They make horror movies about that. Even after his conversion, we still observe some expressive, intense emotion in Paul — such as the anger he expressed toward a group that was trying to sabotage his ministry (Gal. 5:12). Yet, back when God introduced Himself to Paul ("Saul of Tarsus" at the time), did the Lord try to squash Paul's brashness? Did the Potter destroy this aspect of Paul's personality, turning the man into "Paul lite, now with less carbs, less spice, and less emotional energy than before"? No. Rather, God redirected Paul's passion. Beneath the disordered zeal of Paul's former persecution of Christians was a passion that God had instilled. Aimed in the right direction, it helped to drive the apostle to bring the Gospel to the Western Hemisphere. I'm writing this book today thanks in part to the emotionally intense personality of my patron saint.

The Example of Emotional Sensitivity

Parallel to St. Paul's passionate zeal, our own emotional strengths and weaknesses are often the same God-given characteristic in different settings — adopting either disordered or well-ordered expressions, depending on the situation. Take sensitivity, for instance. Do you know any exceptionally *sensitive* people? Are you an emotionally sensitive person yourself? Or, like me, do both statements apply? As any sensitive person — myself included — could tell you, this particular personality trait sometimes coincides with a propensity to overreact, making mountains out of molehills. And, while our incredible spouses are nothing but patient with us in this regard, no doubt our occasional disproportionate responses to situations can be irritating. How could they not be?

In pastoral circumstances, on the one hand, a minister can readily recognize his sensitivity as the strength that it is — a beautiful, God-given characteristic that aids missionaries with natural empathy and compassion for the troubled hearts they serve and comfort. When facing the daily stressors of life, on the other hand, sensitivity may *seem* like an annoying weakness that makes each anxiety feel more unbearable than it needs to feel. In such situations, a sensitive person may even find himself bemoaning his sensitivity, wishing that he "had a thicker skin." The devil may be right there to lie and accuse, trying to get the person to regret how God designed him. The freeing truth is that sensitivity is a God-given gift needed for ministry. The cross that comes with it doesn't change the fact that it's a gift.

Any disordered expressions of it also don't change the fact that the sensitivity itself is a gift from God, integral to a person's finest moments. This trait may coincide with certain problematic disordered manifestations, but the sensitivity itself is not the problem. The key to healing isn't to get rid of something but to bring it into increasing alignment with love—to exercise this God-given gift in well-ordered ways. The trait itself comes from God, and we sensitive folks should thank Him for it.

The Example of the Emotionally Thick-Skinned

Conversely, consider a person who has a thick skin—a natural resilience to stress. This quality is a godsend when it comes to vocations of high-profile leadership; it can help a leader to coordinate the moving pieces of evolving systems and to navigate the host of variant personalities and maturity levels necessarily involved in day-to-day duties. Yet, in the personal exchanges of daily life, this particular trait may coincide with struggles to fully listen, compromising the ability to show the warmth of support first, before rushing to offer solutions.

Whenever such challenges or disordered expressions surface, the resilient person may perceive his resiliency as a problem to be fixed. Yet, he too must realize that it is a gift from God, and that it is likely at the heart of his most significant contributions to the world around him—and so his ability to glorify God. The cross that this hardness entails and any disordered expressions of it do not change the fact that the resiliency itself is a gift—one that the rest of the Mystical Body needs. Without our resilient workers, the work wouldn't get done.

APPLYING THE CONCEPTS ACROSS THE BOARD

Whether you're a sensitive empathizer like Mary or a tough worker like Martha, the body needs you. Taken together, Paul's emotional intensity, people with a sensitive affect, and those with resilient hearts all reinforce the same truth: our feelings are a fundamentally good part of us that we need desperately—both implanted by and reflective of God Himself. As long as we view our inner monkeys as problems, we're still essentially reducing ourselves to problems to be fixed. The foundation for lasting healing is not complete until we understand emotion as part of God's image in us. We need to reach a place where we can appreciate and be at peace with our feelings.

TEN

Making Friends with Our Feelings

The Starvation Diet

INDEED, MY RELATIONSHIP with my emotions needed to change if I was ever going to advance in the healing process. But I wouldn't realize this fact until I attempted one final and extreme assault against them. In other words, as vice continued to fight back, things were about to get worse before they got better.

One day, when I was looking back at the ten-year plateau, the blame I'd been placing on my emotions reached a fevered pitch of absolute resentment against them. I decided to go to war. It seemed my *feelings* were the problem, as they were always getting me into trouble. I thus came to perceive hungry monkey and all of his devious cousins within me such as chocolate-chip-mint monkey and peanut butter monkey as the sole cause of my overweight plight. I concluded the following: "I've got it! I need to *starve my monkeys.*"

No C-Food

Convinced that my natural appetites were the problem, I proceeded to engage in a starvation diet. I consumed roughly 1,000 calories per day or fewer, through foods that were no fun. Most edibles that began with the letter "C" were completely off limits. Chips, crackers, chocolate, cream, cookies, cheese, cereal, and cow were all forbidden. I call it the "no C-food diet," with obvious exceptions like celery. Carrot cake, another considerable weakness of mine, was *doubly* off limits—as was cotton candy (although I never took a liking to it, oddly enough).

Bovine Brotherhood

While I wasn't allowed beef, I sometimes noted that in order to not look like a cow, I needed to eat like one. As I slowly chewed on raw broccoli, leafy greens with no dressing, spinach with no butter or salt, and other grassy cuisine, I felt a sense of sympathetic kinship with vegetarian animals—I began to understand why cows look so miserable. But, with the aid of flavorless turkey dogs, chicken sausages, and raw chickpeas, I reached my goal. I was starving.

Misperceiving Emotion as the Culprit

From the avoidance of all "C-food" to the abundance of field greens, the fed-up and deep-seated resentment of my emotions drove every aspect of the starvation diet. My solution, in short, was to *scorn* my emotions—trying to silence their sway. One trouble with this attempted solution, of course, was that I'd again fallen headlong into treating myself like a problem to be fixed. Another issue was that, ironically, I was trying to destroy my emotions because I was *angry* at them—which is an emotion.

Short-Term Success, Long-Term Failure

One of the dangers of a starvation diet is that it appears to yield fast rewards. As I fit into smaller and smaller clothes, the compliments poured in from friends, family, and neighbors. Funny how, in attempting to starve my passions, I'd apparently left pride monkey off the hit list—I reveled in the compliments.

Anyone who has ever attempted a starvation diet of this nature already knows how the episode ends: (1) the approach isn't sustainable, (2) the wounded self-image beneath obesity never heals, and (3) you gain all the weight back. This trifecta is precisely what happened to me. As I inevitably folded up my skinny clothes to store them away again, and pulled my fat clothes back out, I finally realized that my approach had been flawed. I recognized again, this time to a greater degree than before, that disorder was the problem, not me. I was then able to aim the fight where it belonged: against vice, not against myself.

DISCUSSION

The Influence of Emotions, Both Negative and Positive

As my experience with the failed starvation diet showed me, emotions are potent little buggers. In their disorder, on the one hand, they can cause us the most intense difficulties across the road to healing. Disordered emotions can make a trip to the gym feel arduous to the point of being unbearable. They can make portion control feel like you'll never be happy again. They whine like toddlers deprived of a toy whenever you eat salad instead of late-night junk cereal. And they can make it feel nearly impossible to walk away from excessive peanut butter.

On the other hand, when they are well-ordered, emotions provide powerful help across the healing path. They can make a trip to the gym feel awesome. They can incline you to watch portions — even curb peanut butter intake. They can happily celebrate over the salad as well as the smaller pants sizes that result. Whether harmful or helpful, one thing remains consistent — emotions have a way of making themselves felt.

APPLYING THE CONCEPTS ACROSS THE BOARD

Disordered Feelings: Three Ways Not to Respond

In our fallen state, we inevitably have to deal with disordered appetites. But how? The stories you've heard have already demonstrated a few ways for us *not* to deal with unhealthy feelings, no matter what the struggle happens to be. First, we cannot do whatever our disordered emotions incline us to do. If we do whatever our unexamined feelings say, then we're not free—we've become their slaves. We live in a culture of emotivism that often totalizes the message "follow your heart," telling people to "ignore your head."[1] But this ideology is easy to refute; we can all remember moments in which what we felt like doing was in fact outright harmful—and we ought to have listened to the voice of reason. Doing whatever my emotions told me to do is how I came to weigh over 300 pounds in the first place. Whatever your own healing need, I'm sure you can identify times when misleading feelings led you astray. Clearly, we cannot enslave ourselves to every fleshly urge and expect to be happy.

Second, our response to disordered feelings should not be to destroy them, either. Just as our society includes unbalanced messages that totalize emotion, it sometimes preaches the opposite: telling us to champion their elimination, as I tried to do through my failed starvation diet. By way of example, consider the following sentiment: "Don't let 'em see you cry." Our marriages would definitely not benefit if we kept our deepest joys and sorrows hidden from our spouses in such a way. Refreshingly, Pope John Paul II reminds us that "all that forms the content of the life of married couples must constantly find its full and personal dimension in life together, in behavior, in feelings!"[2] Emotions are, in fact, a crucial part of all types of love—essential to what it means to be human. Regardless of the particular struggle, neglecting our feelings is never the answer. If we try to ignore them, we do so to our own demise.

Third, we cannot deal with unhealthy emotions by performing emotional gymnastics, futilely attempting to "whomp up" some alternative affective state. Have you ever tried to pry yourself out of an emotional state? Have you ever responded to a negative emotion by trying to beat it out of yourself, or force it into some different feeling? "I should *want* to study, I should *feel like* praying, I should be *happy* for my opponent's victory!" Even if we can pull it off—however temporarily—the process is exhausting, draining, and counterproductive. No matter the area for which you seek healing, emotional gymnastics are *not* the way to manage disordered feelings.

Befriending Our Feelings

Full and lasting healing doesn't result from any of these dysfunctional approaches. Rather, healing comes from appreciating our feelings. The first and necessary step to befriending our emotions is for us to accept and embrace them as the God-given part of us that they are. For me, this essential shift in the way I understood my feelings supplied the piece that had been missing from an otherwise solid foundation. It can do the same for you, whatever your particular need.

Finally Ready to Leave the Plateau

Rejecting the false and dangerous notion of myself as a problem to be solved meant embracing each part of my body-soul unity as a fundamentally good and dignified reflection of God's image—including my feelings. From there, God revealed the way to respond to disordered passions and cultivate healthy ones instead—the breakthrough I'd been waiting for, the breakthrough I was now ready for. The following chapters will explore this remedy, which led to the defeat of vice and a life more abundant. During this exploration, we shall revisit the subject of befriending our feelings with some additional and abiding insights.

PART IV

*HEALING
BREAKTHROUGHS
FROM THE HEART OF
THE CHURCH*

ELEVEN

The Way Forward in One Word: Virtue

The Heavenly Spoils of Treasure-Hunting

FOLLOWING THE DISMAL failure of the starvation diet, I immersed myself in the works of various saints and doctors of the Catholic Church who, despite my already having a Ph.D. in Theology, apparently warranted greater attention than I had yet afforded them. These works included Augustine's *Confessions*, Thomas Aquinas's *Summa Theologica*, Teresa of Ávila's *Interior Castle*, and Pope John Paul II's *Faith and Reason*, to name a few. In truth, this immersion was only partially motivated by my intentional and desperate quest for obesity's cure. Primarily, it was an occupational hazard: as a Theology professor, I had to prepare my classes. Regardless of the purity of my initial intentions, however, every bit of the reading helped.

Whether research took the form of devotional time or course preparation, I likened all of it to a treasure hunt. I knew that somewhere within the finest minds and brightest hearts of the Church was the sought-after gemstone—the key to deeper healing: the way forward, off the plateau. After digging long enough, I found it. I remember the moment, feeling like Tolkien's dwarf probably felt when he suddenly unearthed a "great white gem of brilliant translucency" from deep within the heart of the mountain.[1] I found the remedy, and it was not of this world.

The epiphany came through the Dominican, Servais Pinckaers, specifically in his book *The Sources of Christian Ethics*.[2] But, do I credit Fr. Pinckaers, or St. Thomas Aquinas, whose thought Pinckaers was unpacking? Credit also belonged to the other saints and doctors mentioned above, as well as their translators. In my epiphany, I recognized that—from Paul to John Paul II—they had each been saying the same thing. Of course, the ultimate credit belongs to the Holy Spirit, who inspired all of them with this heavenly treasure. It's one of the great joys of the Church, after all, that it's a big family with endless gratitude to go around. So, what exactly was this gem of healing truth, the cure from out of this world? It was, in a single word, virtue.

DISCUSSION

Why Virtue Rests at the Core of Healing

Virtue is absolutely central to healing. As we've seen, when begun at the right starting point, the whole healing process can be understood as God's repairing of His own image of love within us. So how, precisely, does virtue fit in? Why is it essential? The short answer is that virtue is love. Perhaps the simplest way to describe love — yet at the same time the most profound way — is what it means in terms of virtue.

Love and Virtue as Synonymous

St. Paul defines love as a compilation of virtues in his beautiful passage from 1 Corinthians chapter 13, which chart-topping rock songs and secular weddings still quote to this day: love is *patient*, love is *kind*. Patience and kindness are virtues. And this list goes on, for love is also merciful, humble, and courageous. Love is self-controlled in the virtue of temperance. Love is receptive in the virtue of docility. And love honors one's own dignity in the virtue of self-care. Correspondingly, love is not vicious; it is not envious, arrogant, or rude (1 Cor. 13:4–5). Envy, arrogance, and rudeness are all vices.

In my former compartmentalization, I used to envision *love* and *virtue* as separate topics. But this notion could not have been further from the truth. In talking about virtues, we are already talking about love — for the virtues are nothing more or less than love's specific qualities. Like St. Paul before him, St. Augustine also equates the two. Augustine plainly states, "I hold virtue to be nothing else than perfect love of God."[3]

To put it simply, virtues are what love looks like; they're love in action. They're what God is like. God is patient, kind, merciful, meek, wise, and just. Since we are reflections of divine love, virtues signify what we're supposed to look like. We're supposed to be patient, kind, merciful, meek, wise, and just. Returning to our question of why virtue is central to healing, the answer becomes clear. The mending of the human being means the cultivation of that which marks our true humanity — love. Virtue is another word for love.

Human Nature versus Sinful Nature

The logic is simple enough. The problem is that we're so accustomed to reducing ourselves to problems that we've forgotten what it means to *be human*. The oft-used phrase "I'm only human" is an unfortunate one. People typically say it in reference to their disorder — to their sin — as though "human" were a synonym for "sinful." Consider the lyric, "I'm only human, born to make mistakes" from the 1986 song by the band The Human League.[4] If you know it, you may remember that this song does also include some praiseworthy messages of honest confession and humble repentance. The truths conveyed are certainly important ones, which I applaud. That said, that particular line is problematic. According to this statement, original sin, rather than love, is humanity's basic descriptive. In this context, the word "human" means "prone to badness." The enemy would certainly prefer that we neglect God's image and instead view evil as humanity's chief defining attribute. The phrase "human nature" falls prey to similar faulty connotations, in which people often have wickedness in mind whenever they say it.

Refreshingly, the term "humane" — the root of which is the word *human* — seems to have preserved a proper understanding of true *humanity* as something godly. The title Humane Society, for example, doesn't intend to convey an organization "born to make mistakes." Essentially, this confusion of terminology is rooted in mixing up "human nature" with "sinful nature"; our sinful nature is indeed prone to disorder. Yet, our human nature remains a dignified reflection of divine love.

We could correct that song by saying, "I'm sinful, born to make mistakes—yet I'm not only sinful. Fundamentally, I'm human, created to reflect God's image. And, in God's loving mercy and grace I am redeemable, able to heal and live as my Creator intended."[5] With that adjustment, the song's theology would be accurate. Making this corrected lyric fit to the melody is a task I'll leave to the professional musicians.

The Unity of All Virtue

The centrality of virtue accompanied a couple other stimulating insights as well. First of all, I learned that the practice of any one virtue is simultaneously cultivating a multitude of other virtues at the same time. For instance, any actions of self-control—the virtue of temperance—are, at the same time, developing the virtue of prudence, for self-controlled behaviors are wise decisions. Temperance also cultivates fortitude because it takes courage for us to confront the sins that have been dominating us for so long. Justice, mercy, patience, gratitude, and humility—they're all bolstered by the virtue of self-control. These observations demonstrate that all virtues are united by love.[6] Talk about efficiency—if you work on one virtue, then you're working on all of them.

The Golden Mean

In addition, my research in virtue made sense of my journey so far. On the front end of my battle with obesity, the vice of gluttony had pushed me to over 300 pounds of weight. Later, my self-starvation diet had failed miserably. I learned that this swing from one extreme to the other is part and parcel to the realities surrounding virtue, but never actually landing on it.

Aristotle explains that:

> Both excessive and deficient exercise ruin bodily strength, and, similarly, too much or too little eating or drinking ruins health, whereas the proportionate amount produces, increases, and preserves it.[7]

Classically, virtue regards the target of loving excellence in any area of human behavior—the Athenian "Golden Mean" that Aristotle describes above. In other words, virtue is the bullseye between *too much* (excess) and *too little* (deficiency). These excessive and deficient extremes are the vices.

The virtue of courage, for example, is love's mark of excellent behavior between the vice of foolhardiness (overshooting courage) and the vice of cowardice (not having enough courage). The Bible echoes this observation in passages that describe sin as "missing the mark" (Prov. 19:2; Rom. 3:23; Heb. 4:1). Aquinas reinforces this truth when he says that evil "may happen either by their exceeding the measure or by their falling short of it."[8] Through this classic exploration into virtue, God showed me that I had received some experiential training in the whole behavioral spectrum—and that excess and deficiency each made me unhappy.

APPLYING THE CONCEPTS ACROSS THE BOARD

An approach through the lens of virtue to battling whatever you are facing can be extraordinarily clarifying. Personally, it took experiences that had previously stumped me and made sense of them: gluttony was excessive, starvation was deficient, and balanced, moderate ingestion was the virtuous path. Can you remember a parallel swing in your own life from one dysfunctional extreme to another—perhaps from deficiency to excess? Did you fluctuate from indifference toward your neighbors to obsessing over their suffering? Have you gone from apathy to excessive rumination? Have you swung from idleness to workaholism? From "just not caring" to "freaking out"? From self-loathing to an inflated ego? Or perhaps from unsympathetic to consumed? Whatever your particular weaknesses might be, we can all identify this pattern in our own lives in one area or another.

Virtue Brings Clarity

Both deficiency and excess are vicious and destructive forces. They cause harm because we're made of love, and all vice—whether deficient or excessive—misses the mark of love. The good news is that, no matter the sickness, God's love is the cure. Whatever your need, love is at the center, the bullseye. In the case of any dysfunction, there is a corresponding and clarifying virtue, some feature of love, that is being missed by the deficient and excessive counterfeits. As modesty is neither shameless nor bashful, and as justice is neither calloused nor spiteful, the qualities of love supply the desired target. Simply recognizing this truth can bring clarity to your situation—a lighthouse to help guide you out of the fog.

Virtue Is Efficient

Better yet, due to the unity of all virtues, a virtue-centered approach to healing is also efficient. As we said earlier, no matter which virtue you work on, you're developing all the other characteristics of love at the same time. Take a moment to ponder which virtue would increase your own healing and happiness the most. Is it self-control? Or is it patience? What about compassion, gratitude, or generosity? Or would it be the mother of the virtues, humility? Perhaps it would be the courage to conquer either timidity or rashness, or diligence to defeat either laziness or perfectionism. Whether the cause of harm is deficient or excessive, virtue is the remedy, as any single one cultivates the whole breadth of love's terrain. Even if the scope of your own need spans several of these examples and more, you can pick just one virtue to work on; when you work on one of them, you work on all of them — efficient indeed.

Virtue Heals the Person

Without a doubt, a focus upon virtue is both clarifying and efficient. But best of all, it heals. I cannot emphasize enough the treasure that I found in this epiphany: virtues are the specific qualities of love. Thus, by growing in them, we shed the deficient and excessive counterfeits that make us miserable and advance instead in the image that defines us as human beings. The question that naturally follows is, how? Practically speaking, how do we increase in virtue? How do we grow in the attributes of love so that we increasingly reflect God's image, thereby repairing our true humanity? What does this graced healing process look like on a daily basis? The following chapter explores the answer.

TWELVE

Stickers for Grown-ups

The Virtue Chart

WHAT HAVE WE covered thus far? It was an eye-opening break-through from the heart of the Church that revealed to me that virtues were the attributes of love. Consequently, the more virtuous I became, the better I would reflect God's image. But, practically speaking, how would God's grace make this healing possible? What day-to-day steps would I take to grow in virtue? I finally began my departure from the ten-year plateau with my very first smiley-face sticker chart.

This chart was a spreadsheet that tracked daily activities sur-rounding the virtues of temperance in the face of gluttony and fortitude in the face of physical sloth. The days of the week topped seven columns across my spreadsheet. Down the left-hand side of the chart, I listed various duties, such as "treadmill every day," "weight-lifting on Tue & Thurs," and "tiny dinner on Mon, Wed, and Fri." The result was a grid, in which each box corresponded to my performing a virtuous duty on a specific day.

Whenever I was faithful to my obligation on any given day, I stuck a smiley-face sticker in the box. For practices that only applied to certain days of the week, I wrote "N/A" on the days that didn't apply, so as not to confuse them for blank boxes. If I performed the virtuous action on a day that wasn't required, I received a bonus sticker. And, if I missed a day, I didn't apply a sad face—the scream-ing blank box on the spreadsheet said it all.

Identifying the Right Duties

Defining these virtuous activities, I found, was paramount. In order to practice virtue, I needed specific duties related to food choices, portion control, and exercise that pertained to my build, age, and gender—such as my needs for more vegetables in my diet and for aerobic exercise on the treadmill. Furthermore, I needed to identify both actions of *commission*, such as eating breakfast every day—a meal I was prone to skip—and actions of *omission*, such as limiting the amount of cheese I consumed. And, over time, I learned that this undertaking of self-mastery extended beyond weight loss; prayer, sleep, spiritual reading, and enjoyable hobbies were also part of my taking better care of myself.

Identifying the Right Degree of Difficulty

I found it equally crucial to define the right level of difficulty. On the one hand, it's easy to go too lax with these obligations. I discov-ered the hard way that, if the changes are too easy, then they'd have no impact. On the other hand, if the duties are too painstaking, I wouldn't last in performing them. The requirements needed to be challenging, for sure, but they also needed to be realistic. Our heavenly Father doesn't ask a sapling to hold up a tree house.

The Experience of a Chart Off-Target

While I experienced the entire range from *too easy* to *too hard*, I especially erred on the side of changes that were too big. In one of my early charts—which I wrongly crafted without any help—the duties weren't baby steps. Rather, they were giant leaps—beyond the limits of my current willpower.[1] My attempts to live up to this hardcore spreadsheet lasted for a month, and then they backfired in epic fashion. Going too big with these activities can be just as bad as going too small.

Recognizing the Need for Relational Support

What did I do after such missteps? Whether momentarily stumbling or falling headlong, the answer was the same: *pray*. After my failed hardcore chart, for instance, I went to Confession, received the Sacraments, and received the grace of God. Through Him, I could look up, get back up, and not give up.[2]

The failure thus taught me an important lesson: that I couldn't heal in isolation. Created by and for love, the healthy relationships in my life would provide the platform for all transformation. God and my wife—the two bosses of me—were especially important. With their help, I went back to the drawing board and identified better initial steps—not too hard, yet not too soft. I also employed the assistance of a new nutrition counselor, one who took a more integrated approach. Before long, my new chart was just right.

The Experience of a Chart On-Target

The improved spreadsheet was challenging, yet it was the right amount of challenging. It even allowed space for a few treats, which interestingly, I came to enjoy even more in their balance than in former binges. As time went on, each week saw a greater number of smiley faces and fewer blank boxes. I also noticed an increasing number of bonus stickers where an "N/A" used to be. By the end of the month, smiley faces were everywhere.

The Inclusion of Proactive Leisure

Later, I began adding a few leisure activities to my list of virtuous obligations. And, by "leisure," I mean far more than just a break from work—which, as important as breaks are, remain "part of the world of work."[3] Rather, I mean leisure in its own right, as an activity of wonder that helps me to reprioritize. True wonder that is directed toward God as we marvel at the work of His hands, I learned, is a form of adoration—a profound truth that only became real to me when I allowed myself to be filled with it.[4]

One of these wonderful activities regarded a cheap birdfeeder that I set up in the backyard. Weather permitting, several days per week I spent at least fifteen minutes sitting outside, watching the fowl politics surrounding the feeder, and naming the winged critters who visited. I still cannot believe how much fun I have doing this. Some of my regular visitors include "Speckled Peggy," "Brave Ladybird," "Captain Bossy Pants the Interlocutor," and "Steve." It might seem odd that a birdfeeder would help me to pursue virtue, yet it did. Offering a glimpse of Eden, the enjoyment helped me to remember the bigger picture meant for us.

The Stickers Really Help

From the earliest spreadsheets that still needed a lot of fine-tuning to the more polished ones that came later—these sticker charts fostered within me an unprecedented mindfulness and intentionality about my daily behaviors. In addition, they helped to keep me accountable. Most important, at the end of each week, I would take that week's filled-out chart to prayer. The light it shed in this context became an indispensable asset.

Weaknesses and Victories Revealed

The blank boxes revealed where I was struggling. I could then ask God for extra grace in those areas, and exercise wisdom in tweaking my activities according to the right amount of challenge. On the other hand, the colorful smiles, signifying victories, served as motivating indicators of progress. They provided me with occasions to thank God for His healing grace, ask Him for the grace to continue, remember to whom the glory belongs, and experience the joy of gratitude. This was how I got started: prayer and stickers. It's how I still do it to this day.

A Childhood Technique Lives On

It may seem juvenile that a professor in his mid-forties is utilizing the same stickers that my kindergarten teacher once used in teaching me how to remember my phone number and address. Yet, I think it is appropriate. While we may like to fancy ourselves mature, adults need duties to grow, just as little kids do. Grown-ups are just oversized children, after all. The stickers truly help. They're motivating. I may want to ignore my "salad duty" one week, yet I don't — because, darn it, I want my smiley face.

DISCUSSION

Putting Theory into Practice

Beyond the realization of virtue's relevance to healing, all of the studying and reading that I mentioned earlier gave me the practical how-to's which had previously eluded me. In particular, I discovered the need to perform individual, virtuous activities every day in order to reach my goal. These actions, in turn, would be internalized through repetition until they became new tendencies. Ultimately, new virtuous tendencies would unbind me from vice's grip and so would free me to become a better version of myself—someone more reflective of love and, therefore, more completely me. I learned that my role in this transformative process required daily cooperation with God's healing grace, one action at a time. This "hands-on access" to virtue's healing power centered upon a brilliant understanding of it that I had discovered in my continued study: St. Thomas Aquinas's description of virtue as an *operative disposition toward the good*.[5]

Some Good Practical Sense on the Other Side of the Language Barrier

I'm ever-wary of language barriers and the ways they can interfere with healing. For instance, I simply cannot imagine one person saying to another, "I'm thrilled to tell you about how I lost over one hundred pounds—through developing my operative dispositions toward the good!" Since we typically don't talk this way, it becomes easy for us to overlook the very remedies that would save us if we let them.

Perhaps the most significant way that language barriers interfere with healing is by evoking a sense of irrelevance. We assume that, if the language isn't familiar to us, then it doesn't matter to us. The enemy is keen to reinforce this lie, adding that it's the popular language which should occupy our attention.

As a growing Catholic, I often find the opposite to be true. Some of this modern world's most common messages are actually twisted and perpetuate grave disorder, such as the phrases *self-made man, open-mindedness, tolerance,* and *be true to yourself.* Our society even celebrates "pride month"—yet there's no "humility month." Meanwhile, language that sounds relatively unfamiliar to the wider culture designates how God has actually called us to live: *fear of the Lord, foot-washing, pray for those who persecute you,* and *die to yourself.* Clearly, language barriers do not equate to irrelevancy, nor does the absence of such barriers equate to messages worth hearing. A phrase such as *operative disposition toward the good* may sound foreign at first, yet it truly rests at the heart of personal repair.

Virtue as an Operative Disposition toward the Good

Before we suffer a *Summa* headache—the painful brain-throbbing that can occur when reading Church documents and trying to further translate something that's already been translated into English—let's keep it simple. The description of virtue as an "operative disposition toward the good" contains three identifiable parts: "operative," "disposition," and "toward the good." If we look at each part, one at a time, then we can avoid the headache. Better yet, we'll find some good common sense.

We'll unpack the rest of this description of virtue later, but, for now, to call it "operative" is simply to say that love is something you *do.*[6] Virtue requires *operating.* We *perform* virtue. It's an *action.* Again, love is more than a feeling. We have to act—hence the stickers, a visible method of monitoring action that helped me focus on my goodness and wholeness instead of on my problems. *Operative* means we have to do something: virtuous baby steps in these daily situations are precisely where the most powerful healing takes place.

APPLYING THE CONCEPTS ACROSS THE BOARD

Have you been on a plateau in your attempts at healing? Are you ready to move forward? Would you like to give our Lord more ground than you have yet surrendered to Him? Do you want to experience personal healing at unprecedented levels? Grab a pen and a blank piece of paper. Across the top, list the days of the week. Down the left side, list specific responsibilities related to the virtue of your choosing as well as one or two enjoyable leisure activities or hobbies. Attach your spreadsheet to a visible wall or door. And, buy a cheap pack of stickers.

As you craft your own list of virtuous duties, be sure to solicit God's help and the help of at least one close friend or family member. Your activities might take the form of acts of commission. "Pray for fifteen minutes every morning." "Set the alarm for 7:00 a.m. on Mon, Wed, and Fri." "Practice piano for fifteen minutes every Tue and Thurs." "Send someone an encouraging email every Fri." "Tell my wife a specific thing I'm grateful for each day."

Your activities may also be acts of omission. "No video games on Tue, Thurs, and Sun." "No cellphone in bed." "No chocolate Mon through Fri." Virtuous actions may even be situational: "If I feel angry, STOP; don't do anything in that moment—quietly remove myself from the situation until I feel more calm and able to communicate with respectfulness." At the end of each week, take your chart to prayer, file it in a folder, make a new one—edited if need be—then repeat. The stickers will start to add up.

How exciting it is to leave behind the plateau of mere problem-solving! This healing strategy works. It is doable. It does not have to feel overwhelming any longer. Satan wants us to feel paralyzed by fear; he knows that the healed person who increasingly reflects God's image in this world threatens him. In response to the lie of feeling overwhelmed is the freeing truth that, at any point in time, healing comes from just one more baby step in virtue. By God's grace, we *will heal*, one sticker at a time.

THIRTEEN

The Power of Habit

Learning to Brush My Teeth

I VAGUELY REMEMBER learning to brush my teeth. Although the details are cloudy, I can recall clearly that, at first, I didn't feel like doing it. Dad reminded me after breakfast every morning and before bed every night to *brush my teeth*. Because Dad said I had to, I begrudgingly smeared the paste onto my brush and went through all the motions. Self-care didn't yet motivate me, as the maintenance of a healthy mouth didn't so much as blip on my toddler radar. After a while, however, something changed. By repeating the action over and over again, I became inclined to brush my teeth. It had become second nature. In short, brushing had become a habit. This behavioral habit, in turn, came to shape me. That is, I had a healthy mouth. It wasn't just the *behavior* that was healthy. Its habituation eventually made *me* healthy.

Connecting Brushing to Weight Loss

I realized that one of the reasons people must "become like children" in order to enter the kingdom of Heaven (Matt. 18:3) is because the whole salvation process works this way. For me to experience freedom from gluttony and self-starvation—and, more importantly, freedom *for* living more happily—I needed to do the same thing I had done when I learned to brush my teeth. I needed to listen to my (heavenly) Father. I needed to perform my duties, allowing virtuous actions to internalize as habits, and watch as these habits shaped my character according to the qualities of love.

Beginning in Difficulty

By parallel, the first time I went to the gym felt like the first time I had to brush my teeth. I didn't feel like it. The treadmill was boring. The weights smelled bad. The whole experience was as dreadful as I had expected. But I did it because my Father said so.

Likewise, the first time I ate "tiny dinner" was unforgettable, even worse than the gym. Where's the cheese? Where's the sausage? No milkshake? My stomach was still stretched by the portions I'd been having. My body had become accustomed to over 3,000 calories a day, and it had been trained to trigger the sensation of hunger by anything less.

Vices, in a counterfeit of the virtues they miss, also shape us through routine — only they work much faster. Back when I weighed over 300 pounds, I once stopped at the fast-food drive-thru on my commute home from school. This single occurrence was all it took for the behavior to internalize as a regular practice. The virtuous acts on my sticker chart, in contrast, took numerous, hard-won repetitions to become routine. Yet, despite my struggles, I had still habituated brushing as an early form of self-care. I knew that these new self-care duties could go the same way.

The Habit-Formation Process

Throughout my weekly sticker charts, I admittedly backslid a lot. But I didn't quit, and that was everything. With an abundance of prayer, Confession, and love from my relationships, I kept collecting stickers one day at a time. I would swipe my gym membership card and get back on the treadmill, even if I'd skipped for two whole weeks. I would perform my muscle-toning exercises. I would grab the grapefruit instead of the cereal bowl. I would substitute wild rice for pasta.

From Rigor to Routine

The very first time that I set the treadmill to its maximum incline, selected a walking pace, and began "climbing the mountain," I asked myself a question: "Is it always going to feel *this hard*?" As I would come to discover, the answer to this question was: "No—it's only going to feel this hard around thirty more times!" Granted, at that point I had no idea how long it would take me to create the habit. And if I had known, I would only have felt discouraged. I couldn't imagine *one more time* of subjecting myself to this uncomfortable monotony, let alone thirty more times.

Yet, if I really thought about it, that was a mercifully small number of repetitions. Was it really the case that, eventually, it wouldn't seem so awful? I'd spent entire decades—twelve months each year, 365 days in a row—shaping vicious tendencies that had me obese, unhealthy, and unhappy. You mean I could reverse it within only a *few months*? Yes.

The Example of a Whirlpool

The process reminded me of making whirlpools in my grampa's pool. Once the water was flowing in one direction, trying to stop it felt impossible at first. We'd hang onto the side of the pool, trying to push and swim against the current we'd already created—only to be repeatedly sucked under and carried backward. It didn't take any effort to travel in the direction the water was already flowing. In fact, if we wanted to go the way the water was already moving, then we didn't even have to swim. If we did nothing, the momentum would carry us. Yet, if we stuck with moving against the current, even though it seemed impossible initially, we could actually make the whirlpool change in the opposite direction.

The Habit Switch Is Flipped

The twenty-ninth time I swiped my membership card, programmed the treadmill, and started up the mountain, everything felt different. It wasn't arduous anymore. It wasn't miserable. I actually felt like doing it. After that, I found myself looking forward to my workout—anticipating with excitement both the upcoming toxin cleanse from working up a sweat as well as that wonderful, healthy feeling afterward which exercise provides.

My eating habits experienced the same shift. I once thought that sparkling seltzer tasted like soda that had been cursed, doomed to exist as a humiliated mockery of itself. I even felt a little offended by it. Now, I can't get enough. I even lost my taste for certain unhealthy options that I used to crave, such as potato chips, which now feel too greasy. Over time, my stomach shrunk, and so it took less food to make me feel satisfied. I slowed my eating pace, allowing time for my body to send the signal that it was full. And I was finally drinking enough water. The whirlpool's current was beginning to push me in the right direction.

The Joy and Thanksgiving of Getting Off the Plateau

Don't get me wrong, sinful disorder isn't gone—nor do I expect it to disappear on this side of eternity. I'm still tempted, and I still stumble in these areas. The point is that healing was happening! After a while, my weight was again dropping without bouncing back. In fact, my scale never saw 250 again. As with brushing my teeth, new behavior had become routine. This behavioral habit, in turn, was shaping *me*—I was becoming a healthier and happier person.

I was on the treadmill when I realized that the fundamental shift had occurred, and I turned my heart heavenward with a personal thank you. "Saints Paul, Augustine, Aquinas, Teresa of Ávila, and John Paul II, thank you for showing me the centrality of virtue. Thanks specifically, St. Thomas, for writing the *Summa*. I know you called it all 'straw' in the end, but we're really broken down here—and we need the basics first. Thanks for the straw!"[1] Ironic that his *Summa* helped me lose weight, for Thomas was himself a portly fellow.

DISCUSSION

Healing Requires New Dispositions

The entire habit-formation process was another display of the understanding of virtue as an *operative disposition toward the good*. Recall from the previous chapter that my sticker spreadsheets originated as an expression of the first part of this description: virtue's *operative* component, something requiring action. In this chapter, we're exploring the second part: virtue is also a *disposition*. Love, after all, isn't merely something we're forced to do out of obligation. It's something we're *disposed* to do from within.

Regarding virtue's dispositional dimension, Aquinas explains:

> Virtue itself is an ordered *disposition* of the soul ... human virtues are habits ... if the *acts be multiplied* a certain quality is formed in the power which is passive and moved, which quality is called a *habit* ... "Like acts cause like habits."[2]

In other words, virtuous actions aren't just actions. Virtue may start at the operative level, as duties we perform out of obligation, yet it doesn't have to stay there. Rather, the multiplication of actions shapes us by internalizing into a routine that feels second nature—a new *tendency* ... a new *disposition*. Putting the first two parts of this description together, the actions that we perform (virtue's operative aspect) develop through repetition into habitual tendencies (virtue's dispositional aspect).

Virtue Rewires the Brain

An important seventy-five-cent term related to habituation is the "neuroplasticity" of the human brain. Our brains, like persons in their entirety, are dynamic. They are not fixed; rather, they are "neuroplastic"—electrically bendable, shapeable. God designed us in such a way that our freely-chosen behaviors forge synaptic pathways like carved channels, which guide the flow of our neural activity. Through habit formation, these pathways can actually be rerouted.

As neuropsychologist Donald Hebb says, "neurons that fire together wire together."[3] Or as Titus, Nordling, and Vitz observe:

> Dispositions shape, for better or for worse, the person's next act.... The neural connections needed for particular acts form neural dispositions to perform such acts again. A more popular way of referring to this phenomenon is "practice makes perfect."[4]

By grouping our synapses in novel ways, new repeated actions carve fresh neural channels that replace the brain's previous well-worn routes. We experience these new neuropathways as new inclinations. Of course, these new emotional leanings—when virtuous—help us immensely. The less resistant we become to healing and the more disposed we are to living rightly, the more momentum we gain in the right direction.

Virtue Reorders Emotion

Recognizing virtue as a habit unlocked the secret to healing my emotional states, taking the process of working with my feelings to an unprecedented level. For emotions to heal, I needed the habituation process to wean me off my former dependency upon them. I needed to dethrone my feelings—they were to be consultants, not kings.

In order for virtue to take hold, the input of valid feelings needs to be *considered* alongside the input of wise reasoning. But in the end, a healthy choice depends ultimately upon the wise exercise of free will—over and above fulfillment of our base inclinations. Prudence, rather than our whims, must rule the day. The habit-forming effect of repetition can, in turn, bring emotions into alignment with God's joyful plans for our lives. By rewiring the brain, virtuous habituation actually changes the way we feel about our daily activities.

Balancing Emotions with Reason and Free Will

The following synopsis offers a succinct account of how to integrate our feelings into virtuous decision-making in a balanced way—in a manner that doesn't allow them to rule us, yet doesn't resent them, either.

> We must maintain strict governance over our internal movements. This means subordinating the lower, affective ordering to the higher, rational one, which in turn requires a careful balancing of our emotional states. Should the lower, sensitive ordering usurp the higher, rational one, or should reason simply scorn outright our internal attraction to goods of the body, the door swings open to some psychological disorder.... an accomplished human life requires a proper "humanizing" of the passions. It requires the integration of the emotions into the pursuit of the good of reason.[5]

In other words, feelings can no longer function as unchecked dictators over our lives, but we can't ignore them, either. Rather, we must appreciate them and receive their valid input, especially whenever they melt the ice of a cold heart and propel us toward the good. At the same time, we must subordinate their pleadings to the dictates of virtue—choosing the right thing even in those moments when we don't feel like it.

Emotional Health

One of the best parts about keeping emotions in proper balance with reasoning and free will is that their invaluable role isn't diminished. On the contrary, the repeated exercise of virtue frees emotions for their fullest expression. The more our emotional leanings align with what we know to be right, the more they can motivate us to choose the good. And the more that our reasoning, feelings, and free will come into one accord with God's plans for us in this way, the more interior wholeness we experience. Virtuous habituation thus mends the wounds which vice has inflicted upon our body-soul unions.

As we revisit here the lifelong process of acknowledging and appreciating our feelings, we see that virtue is the best medicine for our sin-sick hearts. Recall from our exploration into body-soul unity that well-ordered discernment and decision-making in the soul affects our bodily feelings and drives by forging healthier emotional states which, in turn, assist our spiritual discernment and decision-making, which further helps the body, which further helps the soul, and so on. Habit formation has thus shown us a bit more about how this mutually reinforcing relation between soul and body plays out as we heal. In a nutshell, the new synaptic paths carved by habituation mean feeling better about virtue over time. By God's grace, loving actions do indeed shape healthier attitudes. We can never *feel* our way into a new way of doing; rather, we must *do* our way into a new way of feeling.

The Rapidity of the Growth of Vice and Virtue

As I mentioned earlier, bad habits form so easily, but good habits are challenging to cultivate. Why is it easier for us to "miss the mark" (Prov. 19:2) in either direction, either excessively or deficiently, than to hit the pinnacle of love? The answer is that we all experience a *bent toward the negative*—an inclination in our sinful nature "to follow what is worse rather than what is better," as St. Teresa of Ávila says.[6] I call it the "negativity gravity" of our fallenness.

Fascinatingly, we observe this phenomenon throughout all of creation, every aspect of which was affected by humanity's original rupture with its Creator. For example, any gardener knows that the crops require labor to plow, plant, fertilize, water, prune, and pull the surrounding weeds. The weeds, however, spring up all on their own. On this side of Eden, the crops take work; the weeds need no help. Virtue and vice grow likewise.

Virtuous Habituation Varies from Person to Person

The specific number of repetitions that it takes for behavior to become habitual depends upon the person. Some people form good habits more quickly and easily than others do. From experience, twenty-eight seems to be my number. One study places it at "at least fifty repetitions" for most people to create a new tendency.[7] Another study found that it takes, on average, *sixty-six* days of repeating an action for it to internalize into an "automatic" disposition.[8] Remember, though, that this number is an average; many people took longer—some up to 254 days, to be exact.[9] Whether it takes a person twenty-eight repetitions, fifty, sixty-six, or hundreds, the point is that it takes many repetitions of a virtuous action for it to internalize as second nature. If your number of reps is on the higher side, take heart—for you may be correspondingly less prone to harmful addictions. And you may find that good habits, once formed, are more resistant to backsliding.

Other Considerations

In addition to the nature of the action and the individual, a few other factors affect how quickly habits will form. For instance, consider the reality of intermittent stumbling—which is guaranteed across the road to victory. Whenever faltering is followed by a fast recovery, then the person may altogether avoid slowing the habit-formation process. Yet, if instances of stumbling become persistent, then the momentum can shift in the wrong direction and undo recent progress, reforming bad habits. Falling down isn't the issue. Staying down is.

In addition, healing trajectories such as weight loss that include *both* breaking the bad habits of overeating *and* forging the good habits of portion control and exercise may take a greater number of repetitions than a trajectory against which no bad habits have formed. Furthermore, if the virtuous habit was previously in the person's life, then *reforming* it may take less time than it took to create the habit initially. A virtuous synaptic channel—although abandoned for some time—remains available for rekindling.

Questioning the Results of Clinical Studies That Ignore God

Ultimately, healing is so much about God's assisting grace that I question the results of any psychological studies on habit formation that leave prayer and the Holy Spirit out of the picture. Does it really take sixty-six days to create a healthy disposition? Or, does it take sixty-six days whenever we rely on our own limited and insufficient strength by itself? Such is the disappointing nature of studies that ignore the Almighty. It's as though they say, "Hey, let's do a clinical study and leave God, the most important player, out of it. Hey, these results aren't as promising as we'd hoped." In God's absence, how could the findings of such experiments *not* be skewed?

Before God had laid a new foundation for my healing, self-reliance had gotten me nowhere. Across all the workout videos, gym memberships, and diets that I'd attempted, no good habits lasted. And even after the new foundation had been laid, my progress still hit a plateau. However, following over a decade of foundational work, God led me to a point when it took just twenty-eight actions for me to forge a new and lasting routine. The difference was that an all-powerful Advocate had increasingly opened me up to His grace. Obviously, God Himself is the most important factor of all in habit formation. The process will of course be more difficult when a person refuses available help. Worse than difficult, I would call it *impossible*—for, apart from Christ, we can do nothing (John. 15:5).

APPLYING THE CONCEPTS
ACROSS THE BOARD

In brief, there's no one-size-fits-all formula for this. Whether your brain is very electrically shapeable, or seems more "neuro-*stony*" than "neuro-*plastic*," you can still experience the transformation that new habits can bring. If you pray for fifteen minutes every morning, or send somebody an encouraging email every week, or tell your spouse daily something specific for which you're grateful, then doing so will eventually feel like second nature.

God created us in such a way that repeated actions internalize into tendencies. Disordered emotional states can become reordered to wellness by repeating virtuous actions. We *can* experience ever-increasing inner wholeness, even amidst the growth areas that remain. This virtuous transformation is not a quick fix. It is not easy. It is challenging. You will stumble. It will take time. The pursuit of virtue takes many repetitions before you can experience a new disposition. As Chesterton observes, "Christianity has not been tried and found wanting; it has been found difficult and not tried."[10] However, if you try it, it *will work*.

FOURTEEN

"Toward the Good": Becoming Saints

Our Heavenly Destination: The Angel Oak and the River Bend
I'D LIKE TO pass along two images that capture the goal of saint-hood, i.e., God's intended destination for all mankind. The first is a tree—and not the boring kind. Not too far from where I live, a living treasure exists called the Angel Oak. This remarkable oak tree is over four hundred years old. That's right; this wooden colossus has been alive and growing for more than four centuries. She was once a tiny sapling in that same spot, before this country was even established. Now her shade spans more than 17,000 square feet! Her individual branches are the size of tree trunks themselves, and her living explosion of life offers but a glimpse of what just one of God's creations comes to be in the absence of death. After seeing it, every other oak I've ever seen looks like a baby in contrast. And she's *still growing*.

The Angel Oak has become my personal symbol for achieving sainthood. She is like us; or, at least, what we should be. She is a metaphor for what grace makes possible. Such magnificence offers a clue to what God has in mind for us should we take root in Christ and keep growing in the qualities of love. Can you imagine a human equivalent—a person who *keeps growing*, according to what God intended? I'd venture to say that, after four hundred years of maturing in virtue, I'd feel tempted to worship such a person in all of that splendor.

The Angel Oak reminds me that we are designed for *diviniza-tion*—to become *like God*, to be increasingly perfected in love.[1] That is, we're intended to bear witness to an explosion of life and loveliness that began as a tiny mustard seed of faith. Whenever I look upon this symbol of maturity, and extrapolate what its Creator has in mind for those He crafted after His own likeness, new meaning comes to the verse "no eye has seen, nor ear heard, nor the heart of man conceived, what God has prepared for those who love Him" (1 Cor. 2:9).

The second image that describes the goal of sainthood—one that highlights the call to it—is the bend in a river, a winding stream in a forest. You can follow the water only so far with your natural eyes before the path disappears into some unexplored mystery. During nightfall, you might see the faint light from somebody's cabin or woodland home faded in the distance, visible through the trees.

This distant light seems almost magical as it illumines the evening mist that hovers above the water, imbuing it with a barely discernable glow. When you see the iridescent invitation, you somehow trust that there is just enough light for the next move forward. Yet, you only see the light; you cannot make out its source. Who, in such a moment, would not feel the call to go into the mystery? We carry the hope, as we cautiously make our way forward, that the source of that distant light is a home with no goodbyes.

Mending our relationship with God is ultimately a process of hearing His beckoning call, responding with a *yes*, and taking our boats on the journey toward the light. Sometimes, the guiding light is bright and warm, filling us with excited anticipation about the destination. Other times, it seems to vanish around some dark turn, tempting us to doubt whether we ever saw it. These times are the most important of all, for it is when we cannot rely on our own sight that we must increase our trust in the One calling us.

That enchanted sense of allurement, summoning us forward, shows us one thing for certain: we are not home yet, but we long to be. We are homesick, meant for the place where we're headed. We do not belong to this world. We belong there, to the One who called us. This beautiful destination is sainthood—blissful union with Love Himself, thriving as the people He knit us to be. Mending our relationship with God is an adventure up the winding river toward our true home. The best thing about it is that the One calling us onward is, miraculously, also our copilot along the journey.

The Practical Application of Sainthood to the Healing Process

My appreciation for the goal of sainthood has had a positive impact upon my healing efforts. Time and time again, I'd find myself craving my favorite sweets in excess, wanting to eat large quantities of cheese instead of "tiny dinner," or simply not feeling in the mood to get on the treadmill. Even with new habits helping to propel me in the right direction, it still took constant toil for me to maintain the whirlpool's new current—the negative gravity of sin was forever making itself known. In these moments, the desire to solve a problem was simply not motivating enough. But, whenever I took the time to consciously remember the real purpose of virtue, the happiness that it brings, and God's call for me to live life to the fullest, I'd always find that the Lord's grace was sufficient for me. Across my healing journey, I've thus discovered that the goal of sainthood is not only a future reality. Rather, it moves me, stirs me, and drives me in the present moment—the moment where I encounter God.

The Real "Why"

To this day, I still use the sticker charts to maintain my new habits, watching as these habits continually mold a healthier and happier me, both inside and out. But what really stands out is how much an ever-intensifying excitement about God's destination for me has taken the process to a new level. Across time, the more I kept the goal of sainthood in view, the more I ate well and exercised for the right reason: to become the man God intends me to be.

By appreciating our saintly destination, my efforts gradually stopped representing "personal strides to lose weight" and started to mean something infinitely more meaningful—my cooperation with grace. Beyond losing weight, I was participating with the Lord's work within me. I was allowing God to repair my relationship with Him, clarify my image of Him as the loving Father He is, and thereby heal my self-image.

The realization of my ultimate destination also showed me why previous efforts had left me disappointed. As long as I isolated weight loss as the final goal in and of itself, I would never be satisfied. Yet, the more I extended the process into God's eternal plans for me, the more I became invigorated by a transcendent purpose. Oh, how different it is to internalize virtue in order to increase in love than it is to diet and exercise in order to fix a problem.

The call to become a saint has thereby grounded my entire healing process. Whatever healing you are undertaking, remember that it's one piece of the whole salvation process. It's not that we alleviate our problems and we find advancement in virtue as a nice bonus; it's quite the opposite. As we increase in virtue, God mends His defining image of love within us. The evaporation of our problems is the nice bonus.

DISCUSSION

The Third Piece of Virtue

In unpacking the concise yet profound understanding of virtue as an *operative disposition toward the good*, we've covered the first two parts of this threefold description. Virtue's *operative* part showed us that we need to act—before we feel like it. Virtue's *dispositional* part showed us that these dutiful actions internalize and become habits through repetition, such that we become increasingly inclined to healthier behaviors over time. Now we'll talk about the third part.

Do you recall the story of how I learned to brush my teeth? The process began with actions performed out of obligation, but it didn't stay there. It proceeded into habits, in which repeated actions disposed me to the behavior over time. Yet it didn't stay there, either. In the end, the healthy habits made me into a healthier person. My *actions* formed *habits* that formed *me*. The third part of our description covers the reality that virtue eventually molds the person's character in a well-ordered direction. It aligns us "toward the good." It makes saints.

We Are Becoming Something More

"Toward the good" addresses the direction in which our daily living propels us. Humanity's capacity for *growth*—for change, advancement, development, maturity, and transformation—is a gift that we often take for granted simply because we don't know any other way to be. From the cradle to the grave, we spend our whole lives growing naturally, and hopefully maturing spiritually, too. But, let's stop and marvel at it for a moment, allowing ourselves to be filled with childlike wonder at our Creator's majesty: we are *not* static beings; rather, we either grow, or we decline, across the mysterious stage of time. God made us *dynamic* beings. Pondering the marvel of our existence is already astonishing enough. Yet, beyond the fact that we *are*, there is more — we are also *becoming*.

What exactly we are becoming depends. It depends upon our daily actions — which internalize into routine inclinations, which in turn, shape our character. The "toward the good" piece of the description draws in this reality that our actions and dispositions come to mold who we are across time. It addresses the fulfilling purpose at which virtues aim and therefore the good direction to which virtues impel us. As love grows, we are becoming increasingly well-ordered to the happy purposes for which God created us, the ultimate purpose of which is loving union with Him. In contrast, if we continue in sinful vice — which binds, blinds, and fractures — we are becoming increasingly disordered, oriented away from God's happy plans.

Simply put, the third part of the description regards the observable fact that virtue propels us in a good direction — toward a life that thrives in excellence. St. Thomas explains:

> Human virtue which is an operative habit, is a *good* habit, *productive of good works*; "No one can doubt that *virtue makes the soul exceeding good*."[2]

Those who abide in the various attributes of love are *aimed* toward life to the fullest. We're headed to sainthood!

The Long Road Home

I suppose that, just as we can ask how many actions it takes to generate a habit, we might also ask how long a habit has to persist before it's definitive of the person's character. The lifelong struggle against concupiscence — the *dying to self*, the painstaking mortification of disordered passions, and the sheer challenge of it all — might have us asking, "How long will this take? Why, oh why, does God delay His ultimate gift? Why do I have to wait for it? Why is there such a long and bumpy road to the third stage of virtue?" Pope Benedict XVI offers an anointed answer:

> Man was created for greatness—for God Himself; he was created to be filled by God. But his heart is too small for the greatness to which it is destined. It must be stretched. "By delaying [His gift], God strengthens our desire; through desire He enlarges our soul and by expanding it He increases its capacity [for receiving Him]."[3]

Why does God delay His ultimate gift? Because our hearts are too small, and we would miss out in our incapacity to contain it—God loves us way too much to let this happen. This hope-filled journey stretches our hearts. By enlarging our souls' desire for Him, God increases our hearts' capacities to receive Him. We must be stretched; the lifelong process of healing does just that.

The Relationship between Virtue and Beatitude

In the end, this three-stage healing process of performing duties, internalizing dispositions, and thriving in excellence is none other than a description of *beatitude*. Beatitude is not an exact synonym for virtue, although the two are closely connected—examining this connection is worth a moment of our time. The Beatitudes from Jesus' Sermon on the Mount all *include* virtues (such as mercy and meekness), but what exactly makes a beatitude a beatitude? A beatitude takes a virtue—some quality of love—and extends it over time, to cover the fruits it bears and the blessings God will bestow in the virtuous person's life.

Let's look at an example: "Blessed are the merciful, for they will receive mercy" (Matt. 5:7). If we consider the full proclamation, then we see that Jesus' statement covers a timeline. Those people who presently show the virtue of mercy will be shown it in the future. This whole statement, in its entirety, is a beatitude. In short, virtues are qualities of love, while beatitudes pronounce the blessings that await people who are formed in those qualities of love across the developmental trajectory of their lives.

Whether directly or indirectly, each beatitude includes virtue. Granted, several of the beatitudes do not identify a virtue explicitly, such as "Blessed are those who mourn, for they shall be comforted" and "Blessed are those who are persecuted for righteousness' sake, for theirs is the kingdom of heaven" (Matt. 5:4, 10). "Mourning" and "being persecuted" do not exactly name virtues proper. Nevertheless, each Beatitude clearly describes virtue. In these examples, mourning displays the virtue of compassion, and withstanding persecution for the sake of righteousness exhibits the virtue of fortitude.

The Magna Carta of Christian Living

Jesus' Sermon on the Mount, which lists the Beatitudes, is our Creator's instruction to His creation about how we should live — "the *magna carta* of Gospel morality," as Pope St. John Paul II calls it.[4] And Christ's teaching is markedly unlike the "morality" of today's world in a number of ways. In contrast to modern schooling in ethics, Christ did not stress the politics of His day. His driving question was not, "How far can I go without violating an obligation?" He never treated us as problems to be fixed. And He certainly never said that "having the right information" is enough by itself. It's tragic that our world so often emphasizes current events, rule-breaking, problem-solving, and having the right info — with nary a word about beatitude. The enemy doesn't just counter Jesus' teaching by attacking it directly; he also attacks it by training us to not even consider it.

When God taught us how to live, He taught beatitude. That is, He stressed the importance of living virtuously and the promises in store for those who do. Look at it this way: God Almighty walked the earth at one point, revealing to His creation what He wants us to grasp at this point in our existence. By analogy, imagine a computer programmer actually showing up inside his own program. The characters he designed would do well to hear whatever their programmer had to say.[5] While He was here enfleshed among us, God incarnate blessed us with teaching about how He wants us to live—clear guidance about how exactly to heal. We would be wise to listen.

APPLYING THE CONCEPTS ACROSS THE BOARD

The operation, disposition, and mature freedom stages of developing virtue are themselves the path of beatitude. Across these chapters, we have been describing how love's qualities grow from duty to habit to mature excellence—and the happiness that awaits those who follow this graced path. We've been describing beatitude, the nuts and bolts of salvation broadly speaking. No matter the need, the healing process remains the same: repeated acts of love internalize into loving dispositions that mold a lovely person. By following this three-stage healing process, we are following our Lord's instructions on how to reach the joy of sainthood.

Because Christ defeated death, we can thrive in this life and beyond by increasingly becoming who we were created to be. We do this by saying yes to His grace and maturing in the various qualities of love—these *operative dispositions toward the good* known as virtues—as God assists us along the way through His presence in the Sacraments, in prayer, in others, and in us. Indeed, happy are those who hunger and thirst to live virtuously, "for they will be filled" (Matt. 5:6). Through the three phases of love's development, God will heal us. Then, like a stained-glass window—broken pieces made into stunning works of art—our own redeemed brokenness will illumine for all eternity the unbound love of our sovereign God.

PART V

ABIDING

IN VICTORY

FROM HERE

FORWARD

FIFTEEN

The Daily Struggle

From the Mountaintop to the Valley

Discussing our blessed destination in the previous chapter offered us a hope-filled panoramic of the whole forest—a breathtaking God's-eye view of where the salvation process is taking us. It is motivating, as it ought to be! At the same time, we're not there yet. We're still down here, lost in the mundane consequences of our exile, navigating the cares that hijack our focus, and repeatedly losing sight of the prize. Like Bilbo who got a brief look from the treetops of Mirkwood, we too must descend back down into the dark forest in order to advance farther along the trail, trying to remember what we saw as we go.[1] This exploration into healing wouldn't be complete if I only discussed the good, then glossed over the intense challenges we face along every stage of beatitude's path.

On the Upside: A Characteristic Example of a Good Day

I'll begin with the good. I attended a birthday party recently, and the people who organized my friend's celebration spared no expense. In addition to the presents and games, there was a lot of good food—and free booze. But the party just so happened to fall on a day that required tiny dinner, no sweets, and no nightcaps. Caving in would have been easy, of course. I could always swap that particular day's duties for another day during the same week. I wouldn't even call such a course of action sinful.

Instead of choosing the comfortable option, I stopped for a moment and thought about my choice. I consulted both my emotions and my reason. I was careful not to silence or resent my feelings—while still subordinating their pleas to wisdom. I was aware that I felt tempted to gluttony, which would of course be wrong. At the same time, I was also aware that the bodily enjoyment of good food is not wrong in and of itself. I discerned that enjoying a reasonable portion of rich food and strong drink constituted a viable option. However, I also knew that the most excellent option would be for me to stay faithful to my sticker chart.

With all of these considerations rapidly undertaken, I said a prayer for grace, drank water instead of beer, ate a small salad for dinner, and distracted myself from the buffet by playing water balloons with an adorable toddler. Later that night, as I applied the stickers to my chart, my decision filled me with encouragement, confidence, and gratitude for God's help. That was a good day.

On the Downside: A Characteristic Example of a Bad Day

On the other hand, slipping up still happens. Not too long ago, I reviewed my chart in the morning to see which duties were on the docket for that day. "Let me see here, we've got another round of tiny dinner, no sweets, and no nightcaps today—I'm good to go on all those. I'm also supposed to pray outside while watching the birds chow down at the peanut feeder—that's always fun. But, what's this . . . a treadmill day? Ugh. For some reason, I *really* don't feel like 'climbing the mountain' today."

Even though my workout schedule had become routine at this point in my life, my inner lazy monkey threw one of his occasional fits about exercising. It still happens from time to time that my well-formed dispositions seem to vanish, as my flesh betrays me to old itches. Such times are none other than manifestations of the sinful disorder within us, and they are to be expected.

Maybe I woke up on the wrong side of the bed that day. Or perhaps I was under one of those trials inflicted by the enemy, which St. Peter warns us about. He says, "Beloved, do not be surprised at the fiery ordeal that is taking place among you to test you, as though something strange were happening to you" (1 Pet. 4:12). Whatever the reason, in the irrationality of vice, I chose to neglect my duty that day, then the next day, and the next. Before long, four weeks of blank treadmill boxes on my charts and five more pounds resulted. "One tiny little choice" had launched a domino effect of vicious formation in the wrong direction, as I repeated the failure enough times for bad habits to reform.

Healing Is a Messy Endeavor

If you were to graph my progress on a Cartesian plane in which the X-axis represents time and the Y-axis represents my growth in charity, the points that take me from "first starting out" to "where I am now" do *not* connect into a straight diagonal line nor a tidy upward curve. Instead, my graph looks like a squiggly muddle that goes into other quadrants, off the paper, and even into other dimensions. The squiggly shamble looks like a blob. The blob, however, generally moves up over time. By grace, it has adopted an observable upward slope.

I know I'm not alone in the messiness of the healing process. St. Paul admitted that he presses on toward a goal not yet reached (Phil. 3:12). He said, as we've mentioned before, that he struggles in doing what he shouldn't while not doing what he should (Rom. 7:15–19). St. John admitted that, if we say that we are *without* sin, then we're lying to ourselves (1 John 1:8). As Jesus warned, "the spirit indeed is willing, but the flesh is weak" (RSV Matt. 26:41). Being perfected in love by God's grace is a rough and blundering ascent. But, through grace, ascend we can.

DISCUSSION

Remembering the Foundation

Examples of the good and bad can shed light upon what the salvation process looks like as we work it out "with fear and trembling" (Phil. 2:12). In particular, these experiences demonstrate our everyday participation—or lack thereof—in God's healing work. Foremost, as we abide in the ongoing process of healing from this point forward, it is outright crucial that we remember the foundation.

To review, we must first always bear in mind that our heavenly Father lays the groundwork for human healing, not "problem-solving." We are not the problem—sin is. Sin is not sovereign—God is. In truth, we are a reflection of divine love, and, in His mercy, the Lord has made redemption available. In short, the problem is not the foundation—God is. Second, in order to receive the Lord's grace, we need to humble ourselves before Him. We need to recognize who we truly are, recognize the sin within us that attacks who we truly are, and humbly receive the love that saves us. Third, we must pray. This vital communication link between ourselves and God is essential to life.

This groundwork undergirds every subsequent phase of healing. As you cannot build a good house atop a faulty foundation, a successful healing process must remain grounded upon these fundamentals. If somebody reduces himself to a problem, refuses to humbly receive from God and neighbor, or ignores the guidance of the Holy Spirit, then sticker charts won't amount to a hill of decaf beans. When it comes to our daily participation in God's healing work, first and foremost we must remember the foundational elements of our faith. "Unless the Lord builds the house, those who build it labor in vain" (Ps. 127:1).

Practicing Mindfulness in Our Day-to-Day Choices

Second, we must make mindful choices, both prayerful and intentional — not merely react to emotional impulses by themselves. In the face of day-to-day hankerings, we need to take a moment to move beyond our reflexes in order to distinguish healthy options from harmful ones.[2] That is, we need to take a momentary step outside ourselves. By doing so, we remove the blinders of vice, we see more clearly, and then we can make free choices — as opposed to remaining enslaved to disordered cravings and impulses.[3]

In acknowledging and accepting our feelings, we should both appreciate and consult emotions, absolutely; but, in the end, wisdom should lead the way. Simply put, we all need to take a moment to step outside ourselves, examine our daily decisions, and choose the right baby step. Beware of running on "autopilot." As my testimony demonstrates, it's when we stop being intentional about what we do — and merely react instead — that the healing process goes awry.

Respecting the Formative Nature of Each "Little Decision"

Third, when it comes to the daily struggles of healing, there is no such thing as "just one tiny little choice." Virtue's three-stage path has shown me that any seemingly small decision is internalizing and molding me, propelling me toward whatever the action is aimed at accomplishing. Every day, my individual choices are forming the man I am becoming. Whatever I do shapes me.

When it comes to healing in virtue and living as people who reflect God's image, our daily choices are where it happens. Not surprisingly, when it comes to performing our daily responsibilities, Satan lies and says, "This action isn't going to help you — it's just one tiny little choice." Likewise, when it comes to temptations to vice, he lies and says, "This action isn't going to hurt you — it's just one little decision." In either case, you can call upon the Lord in response, praying with the conviction of truth: "There's no such thing."

Facing the Fight Thru's

Finally, we cannot discuss our daily struggles without addressing the toughest sort. Across every stage of the healing process—from first operating in virtue before we feel like it, to experiencing new virtuous habits, to thriving in excellence—certain decision-making moments are going to feel unusually difficult. Such moments aren't just hard; they seem impossible. Regarding his own initiation into Christ's salvation process, Augustine vividly recalls:

> My one-time mistresses held me back, plucking at my garment of flesh and murmuring softly: "Are you sending us away?" and "From this moment shall we not be with you, now or forever?" And, "From this moment shall this or that not be allowed you, now or forever?" ... the strong force of habit said to me: "Do you think you can live without them?"[4]

As we heal, we too can expect to hear our bad habits insist that we cannot live without them. I've heard the especially challenging occasions referred to as "fight thru's".[5]

Why Fight Thru's Are Opportunities

The good news is that the hardest times are precisely where the greatest healing happens. For one, winning the fight thru's accelerates the habit-formation process more so than the making of relatively less difficult decisions. One specialist says, "The key to moving to the [next] phase of habit formation [a behavior feeling like second nature] is to win two or three 'fight thru's'. This is critical."[6] More importantly, at any stage of virtue's development, winning a fight thru is an act of loving God with all our heart. Jesus said, "If you love me, you will keep my commandments" (John 14:15). Each individual action of obedience, especially during our worst trials, says "I love you" to God. In Christ, the toughest times are recast not as moments to fear, but as the most fruitful of opportunities. Our Redeemer has again turned the worst into the best.

How to Win the Fight Thru's

How do we attain victory during our most trying moments? It may seem counterintuitive, but winning these battles is mostly a passive endeavor. After St. Augustine describes his own fight thru, he offers us a powerful prayer that captures this reality:

> Why do you stand upon yourself and so not stand at all? Cast yourself upon Him and be not afraid; He will not draw away and let you fall. Cast yourself without fear, He will receive you and heal you.[7]

This moving illustration captures a trust-fall upon the Redeemer. Augustine doesn't describe a proactive brand of combat in which the sinner defeats his own sin through sheer willpower alone. Instead, he describes "letting go." We find a similar image in Moses, when he was so weary that he couldn't even hold his own arms up—needing Aaron and Hur to hold them up for him (Exod. 17:12).

APPLYING THE CONCEPTS ACROSS THE BOARD

Relatedly, consider a man addicted to pornography who engages the healing process and faces a fight thru in his virtuous habit formation. He'll get far more mileage out of praying, cutting the internet connection to his house, and turning to healthy friendships than from sitting there saying, "I'm not going to do this, I'm not going to do this, I'm not going to do this"—until his own tired arms lose their strength and fall, with nobody there to catch them. The man should avoid circumstances that render him vulnerable to the vice, as much as it's possible to do so. Jesus *wants* us to fall upon Him. He *wants* to hold our arms up. He *will* receive us and heal us. He never asked us to bear the burden alone. He doesn't want it to be grueling for us to heal.

Avoiding Sin's Occasion

At any degree of difficulty, much of the battle regards relying upon God's grace to "lead us not into temptation" (Matt. 6:13). As Sirach says, "Turn away your eyes from a shapely woman, and do not look intently at beauty belonging to another; many have been misled by a woman's beauty, and by it passion is kindled like a fire" (9:8). Jesus expresses a similar instruction with His vivid metaphor that "if your right hand causes you to sin, cut it off and throw it away; it is better that you lose one of your members than that your whole body go into hell" (Matt. 5:30). Pope Gregory XVI echoes this truth, reminding us "to avoid not only sins but the next occasion of sin as well."[8]

Cut the internet connection if you need to, don't have vodka in the house if it will cause you to stumble, and don't keep cookie dough in the fridge to begin with. Fiery trials *will* come—but let's not make it harder than it needs to be.

Accumulating the Victories

When it comes to experiencing victory in the daily struggle, we find the best image of all in Christ Jesus Himself when He faced the lust of the eyes, the lust of the flesh, and the pride of life in the wilderness (Luke 4:1–13). Jesus remained faithful in His battles by turning to God, quoting God's Word, and resisting the evil one. By the grace of God, we can do likewise. And as James 4:7 pronounces, when we resist the devil, he *will flee.*

Whatever virtue you're developing, you will have good days, thanks be to God. Inevitably, the healing path will include some intensive wilderness experiences, too. Across the entire process—as you repeat actions of virtue, which internalize as habits over time, then eventually shape your character—a few basic reminders may continually benefit you as they have me. First, remember that God is the foundation. Second, be mindful about your daily decisions. Third, respect the formative nature of each individual decision, aware that there's no such thing as one tiny, little choice. Finally, recognize the hardest battles as the greatest opportunities. These reminders can help keep the stickers coming; each one is a victory.

Receiving those stickers isn't easy, but, through the cultivation of virtue, you will experience the new habits and renewed character that you seek. This is good news—the day-to-day victories of your baby steps are *cumulative,* resulting in unprecedented transformation. In the end, you will find that our God is bigger than the daily struggle.

SIXTEEN

Maintaining the Elusive Virtue

An Unforgettable Shopping Experience

BACK WHEN I first hit the 250-pound plateau, I needed a new wardrobe; none of my 300-pound clothes fit me anymore. As I went dancing up and down the aisles of a Ross Dress for Less, tossing new jeans and shirts into my shopping basket, I felt a tap on my shoulder. I turned to see an effervescent woman who was an unforgettable caricature of herself. She stood there for a moment, wearing a concerned facial expression. The exchanges that followed illumine why I stayed on the plateau.

"Break-up?" she asked.

I answered, "Sure, we can break up. I didn't realize we were dating, and I have to say that was the shortest relationship of my life—but yeah, sure, we can break up."

"You're funny!" she replied. "Seriously, I see a guy who is shopping like a girl, and I just have to wonder—do you have a broken heart, and are you dumping a bunch of purchasing on top of your pain?"

I responded, "How considerate of you, thank you for asking. I'm delighted to report that this is actually happy shopping, not coping. I lost a bunch of weight."

"Oooo, how much?!" she enthusiastically interjected.

"Somewhere between forty and fifty pounds so far, but I need to ..."

She interrupted me again, "What was it? Wait, no, don't tell me. I want to guess. Guessing game! [She abruptly clapped her hands three times.] Was it the Atkins Diet?"

"No, it was ..."

"Please, let me guess!" she insisted. "Was it South Beach?"

I shook my head. Next, she suggested, "Wait a minute, it was that low-carb, no-carb plan, wasn't it? No? ... how about Weight Watchers? Still not right? I've got it—Richard Simmons' videos! No? I give up—WHAT WAS IT?"

"It wasn't anything," I said, "just the 'Ian Diet,' I guess."

With the intensity of slow and purposed speech, she implored, "Tell me of this *Ian Diet*."

I answered, "Oh, it's not a genuine diet plan, I was just trying to be funny. 'Ian' is my name ..."

"I realize you were joking," she said. "You lost over forty pounds, so you can call it whatever you want. Just, you must tell me how you did this."

I explained, "There really was no gimmick. I ate less ..."

"*Uh huh*," she interjected, with a note of desperation in her voice.

I continued, "... and I exercised."

"*Yeah?*" she replied, with an eager and questioning tone that obviously expected to hear more.

"And that's it," I said. "I ate less, and I exercised."

She responded, "That doesn't work, does it?"

"Yes," I replied, "It works. In fact, it's guaranteed to work. If you're *burning* more calories than you're *taking in*, then biochemically speaking, you will lose weight. It's impossible not to."

"It's so simple, it's genius! The gimmick is *there is no gimmick*. Don't go anywhere, I'll be right back."

She brought her daughter back, and almost the exact same conversation played over again. Then a man who happened to overhear us stepped over, asking apologetically if he too could learn the secrets of the Ian Diet.

By this time, I was imagining the book tour after my Ian Diet topped the *New York Times* bestseller list. What a trip.

Lessons from the Shopping Experience

These memorable exchanges marked a prodigious moment in my journey; however, it highlighted sinful pride within myself, at the same time. On the one hand, strangers at a clothing store started humbly sharing their struggles, receiving from their neighbors, and inspiring one another. Also, the episode was an experience of early success, which showed me that weight loss was feasible. My encounters with these three bright individuals inspired me, and our dialogues were undeniably hilarious. These aspects of the day were all good ones. On the other hand, I had been overtly naïve to think that the substantial healing I sought was simple and achievable by my willpower alone.

In hindsight, I see an obvious arrogance in my attitude that I'd purported to discover some brilliant simplicity overlooked by everybody else. If weight loss was truly a simple matter of eating less and exercising, as I had made it out to be, then why would I remain stuck hovering around the 250-pound mark for years to come? In truth, healing from gluttony (and for health) is not simple. It's not simple because it's not just our bodies that need to heal. Interestingly, in taking credit for my progress thus far, my progress stopped.

An Unforgettable Classroom Experience

Years later, while teaching an Ethics class, I stumbled across a practical way in which I could maintain and cultivate the humility I needed in order to keep healing past the plateau. In one particular lecture,

I described the three stages of virtue to my students. I explained each phase of our growth in love from (1) performing virtuous duties until they internalize, to (2) maintaining these new habitual tendencies as they shape a good character, to (3) thriving in mature freedom. I then asked the class—one student at a time—at which of these stages of character development they believed themselves to be.

All the students fancied themselves to be at the third stage. They claimed to be pulled by excellence from within, rather than pushed by external, obligatory incentives. They claimed to be beyond the need for duty, no longer internalizing virtuous dispositions but already securely formed in them and enjoying maturity. In effect, they were all claiming to be saints. What they didn't realize was that I knew they would say this, as I once suffered from "young man's disease" myself. In fact, my intentional set-up for this day's lesson had been a couple of weeks in the making. They had walked right into a teaching trap.

Two weeks earlier, I had announced on a Friday that there would be no reading quiz that upcoming Monday. I added, "Class, still do the required reading assigned on your syllabus for Monday, for the sake of excellence in learning. However, you may all enjoy the absence of 'quiz anxiety' across the weekend. Enjoy your time off, and enjoy your readings—free of any grading stress." They were happy students! Teaching is the only market I've found where the customers are the happiest whenever you don't give them what they're paying for.

One week later, I made a different announcement at the end of Friday's class. "There will be a reading quiz this Monday. The quiz will be relatively easy. It's designed in such a way that, if you do the required readings from your syllabus, then you should do well on the quiz. Its object is simply to make sure that you're doing your assigned readings." My students preferred hearing the previous week's announcement that there would be no quiz on Monday. But at least they appreciated the heads-up.

On the day when everybody deemed themselves to have arrived at the saintly third stage, my set-up came to its fruition. I began, "So, you all believe yourselves to be mature, driven by excellence for the sake of love. You no longer need disciplinary duties, and your loving dispositions have internalized to the point of defining a virtuous, charitable, and godly character. Is this accurate?"

Everyone in class nodded.

Smiling delightedly to myself, I then said, "Let me ask you this: a couple of weeks ago, when I announced that there would be no quiz on Monday and asked you to do your readings for the sake of excellence itself, how many of you did the readings? Be honest."

I could literally see the lights come on, in each face in the room. Only one girl raised her hand; she was the only one who had read those particular assignments.

I said, "Very good — thank you everyone for your honesty and courage, two beautiful virtues. I'm not upset with any of you. Actually, I'm rather proud of you for your authenticity. And Heather, thank you for doing the readings — I'll get back to you in a moment. New question: how many people did the readings last week, when I promised a quiz that upcoming Monday?"

All the students raised their hands.

I said, "Thank you, you can put your hands down now. Thanks for doing the readings — you did your virtuous duty that weekend, displaying the virtues of obedience, diligence, and studiousness. And it showed in your grades, which were excellent on that quiz. You have my gratitude. And — I hope you can now see that I set you up."

From the smiles to more nodding heads, I could tell that everyone was tracking.

I explained, "Class, today's point is simple. Most of us have *not* reached maturity in our true humanity and purpose for living. Most of us are *immature* — in most areas of our lives. To explain, when it was for excellence, you didn't do the readings. The disposition to studiousness hasn't internalized yet, as evidenced by the fact that you only read your assignments when an upcoming quiz imposed an external obligation upon you. This clearly indicates Stage One."

Everybody agreed.

I continued, "Yet we all *prefer* to think of ourselves as having reached maturity. Our sinful pride has disordered us according to a distorted perception of ourselves. Like a devious carnival mirror that makes us appear taller and sleeker than we really are, our self-understanding is skewed. We'll even switch back and forth between an *inflated* self-image, like the one we fell into a moment ago in fancying ourselves mature, and a *deflated* self-image, in which we beat ourselves down in self-loathing. The sense of deflation works like another devious carnival mirror — one that makes us appear smaller and fatter than we actually are. From arrogance to insecurity, neither mirror is accurate. Both display a warped self-image."

Heads continued nodding with intense accord.

"So, let's lose the ego of fancying ourselves saints before we are, and let's also lose the insecurity of feeling like garbage. We can be *accurate* with ourselves and with one another that most of us are still beginners. Because here's the deal: the disorder is not sovereign. God is. And through the three stages of character formation, virtuous duties will internalize into habitual tendencies that eventually shape you according to the image that truly defines you — according to love. This healing process begins with Stage One: the repeat operation of virtuous duties. It's a *good* place to be!"

The class looked both relieved and excited, as though scales were falling from eyes and hearts were set free.

I added, "Now Heather, do we have somebody among us who has reached Stage Two?"

Sheepishly, she replied, "No. My motive for doing the readings when there would be no quiz was that I knew nobody else would—and I like to feel superior. My action wasn't really diligence. It was showing off. I do apologize, now that I see it. I want to be better."

The entire class burst out in laughter including Heather, able to laugh at herself as she held her blushing face in her hands and shook her head. Her supportive classmates rallied behind her along with me, impressed by her humble and erudite confession.

One student said, "I do the same thing!"

Another student said, "I'm really starting to get this stuff. Morality isn't just 'a field of study'. Virtuous living is *everything*. It's about becoming loving, and therefore more fully human—and happy. I get it!"

It was a beautiful day—the sort of classroom exchange that a teacher lives for. We were accurate with God, one another, and ourselves, and this community-wide humility had us all celebrating the grace that makes healing truly available. Truth really does set us free.

Lessons from the Classroom Experience

I took this day's lesson into my weight-loss journey by making it a point to stay honest with God in prayer—and honest with myself—about where I was in the process. By being truthful that I'm in Stage Two, I get to celebrate the victory thus far, maintain a cautious awareness of my own frailty, remain grateful for God's strength, recognize my total dependency on grace, and get excited about what's to come, all at the same time.

Authentic self-assessment has thus provided me with a hands-on way to foster the humble spirit God desires. Since all virtues are connected, as I grew in humility in this way, I was concurrently growing in self-care.[1] Between these two properties of love, increased humility brought deeper happiness.

DISCUSSION

Returning to the Mother of All Virtue

As our healing expedition nears its summit, we return now to the "mother of all virtues"[2]—a fundamental piece of this exploration that warrants further attention. Humility is indeed crucial across each stage of the healing process. From first performing duties before we're so inclined, to continually reinforcing virtuous habits once formed, to thriving in saintly excellence, humility remains requisite to each phase. In a sense, she's the lynchpin of the entire healing process; if we cease to be humble, then every truth we've explored will be lost to the blind insanity of arrogance. In contrast, if we embrace her, then the mother of all virtue will continue to produce in our hearts the offspring of self-care, self-control, wisdom, and every other virtue. Unfortunate to this end, however, humility is just as elusive as she is essential.

Humility Is Elusive

Our journey has already seen a number of different portrayals of humility along the way, including receptivity, accuracy, the foundation, and the mother of all virtues. It seems there's no end to the descriptions we can apply to this uniquely attractive attribute of love. Adding to this list, humility has also been called the *elusive virtue*: as soon as you realize that you possess it, you sound less humble.[3]

To explain, as soon as we identify humility in ourselves and take delight in it, we flirt with losing it. Our identification of the possession of humility can tempt us to presume that we fully understand it, offering us a false sense of control. Our delight in it can tempt us to take credit. Presumption, illusions of control, and vainglory—these are all symptoms of sinful pride. If we fall into arrogance, then we have by definition lost humility.

Humility: Rejoicing in It and Seeking It

Within Aquinas's understanding of the good kind of pride, there is room for us to realize and take delight in being humble without losing the virtue in the process—in a manner that magnifies God in gratitude for the saving work He is doing within us.[4] At the same time, we must be aware that taking proper pride in being humble is slippery ground. Even within bounds, standing on slippery ground should make us uneasy.

Aside from the uneasy matter of rejoicing in humility, we can be completely comfortable with *seeking* it. As our reception of the Potter's molding process, we cannot heal without humility. As "the truth that sets us free," it is the spiritual antidote for sinful pride. It heals our misplaced sense of self-reliance. It removes presumption. By realigning us with accuracy, humility cures both the inflated and deflated distortions that covenant-rupture causes. That is, humility increasingly corrects our distorted perceptions of God, and therefore simultaneously cures our warped perceptions of others and ourselves made in His image. And, in its emphasis on receiving, humility can cure the spiritual asthma that might be preventing any healing in us. For all of these reasons, we should always be comfortable seeking humility.

Pray for Humility, No Matter What They Say

I've heard people say, "Never pray for humility or patience, because God will answer." It's as though they're saying, "Beware: if you ask for humility, don't be surprised when God allows the *humiliations* that foster it. Similarly, if you ask for patience, God will allow situations that *try your patience* in order to stretch it." I get it—humiliation isn't pleasant at the time; neither is having our patience tested.

Nonetheless, I say, "Definitely pray for both virtues, *especially humility*." God's response won't stop with humiliations and trials—He promises abundant life! The Beatitudes don't say, "Cursed are the poor in spirit, for theirs is a bunch of humiliations." As Jesus explained, the heavenly Father doesn't have scorpions for His kids (Luke 11:12). Pray for humility. You won't be sorry you did.

APPLYING THE CONCEPTS ACROSS THE BOARD

As the experience in my Ethics class showed, authentic self-confrontation offers us all a way to maintain humility. Namely, we need to keep being accurate with ourselves about where we are in the process, knowing God loves us unconditionally and that He will bring to completion the good work He began (Phil. 1:6). And, although we've certainly not reached charity's perfection, we need to remember that God's grace is sufficient throughout all our stumbling (2 Cor. 12:9)—as long as we continue to "press on" (Phil. 3:12). Being truthful with ourselves in this way, neither inflated nor deflated, is paramount. The assurance of God's love is what makes such honest self-assessment possible; if we forget God's love for us, then our remaining disorder becomes too unbearable to confront.[5]

The Take-Home Message

In summary, humility grows like any quality of love: through mindfully-discerned daily actions that eventually internalize into habitual dispositions, which ultimately perfect a person's character. But what does this process look like at a practical level? How can we—in light of humility's elusive nature—seek this indispensable quality, embrace it, and keep it close? One surefire way is by staying honest that we're still at the immature or intermediate stages in most areas of our life—we still need stickers.

SEVENTEEN

Tying It All Together

The Accuser's Lie and God's Reply

THE SERPENT SAID to me, "Did God really say that that you're never allowed to eat any delicious food? You will surely not die if you eat outrageous portions of carrot cake on a regular basis. First, think how hungry you are. Second, just look at its pleasing, colorful appearance. Third, if you want to eat all of it, then you should. It's *your* life—you only live once."

I saw that the cake looked good for food, pleasing to my eyes, and desirable for my life. And so, I ate all of it. Then I realized that, in overeating, I had actually been unfaithful to my true self—and to others. I broke God's heart, the hearts of those who care about me, and my own heart, too. And rather than standing by me, the serpent turned and said, "You didn't even fight back. You're pathetic. How could anyone love you? How could God love you?"

Liar.

God *does* love us. He showed the world just how much in an act of self-donation that has stumped mortal understanding for the past two thousand years and counting. Our present exploration into healing has been about allowing this infinite love into our own finite hearts, then watching it geyser into transformation and happiness we never imagined possible.

An Overview

My healing journey began with the shortsighted gimmicks of the secular self-help realm. Although well-intentioned, these limited strategies were crippled by the arrogant notion that people can save themselves. Confusing one slice of the picture for the whole loaf, the methods born out of this incompleteness proved unfruitful.

Thankfully, my entry into the Catholic Church provided a new foundation. Initially, RCIA's fundamentals about God's sovereignty over the problem, lessons in humility, and a deepened prayer life combined to launch my healing. This more complete picture addressed not only my physical but also my spiritual needs—and knocked off the first fifty pounds of sustained weight loss. Moreover, both humility and prayer highlighted the vital role of my relationships—I couldn't heal without them, and I needed to humbly receive from God and neighbor. Overall, it was a beautiful time of discovering that sin does not define me.

While this initial layer had started the process, progress froze at a 250-pound plateau across a decade of fighting with my emotions. Misperceiving emotion as the bad guy, I was inadvertently still reducing myself to a problem. But eventually, God showed me that a recognition of His sovereignty included the realization that my emotions weren't problems to be fixed—they were part of His defining image within me. With the entire basic foundation now complete, I was finally positioned to get off the plateau and take the process to a deeper level. That is, I was now ready for breakthroughs from the heart of the Church—epiphanies about the pivotal importance of virtue to healing and the practical steps of its development.

Specifically, by the grace of God, I came across the truth that virtue characterizes love and is therefore the key to human healing. Moreover, I encountered a threefold description of virtue that put it into practice. Initially, accountability spreadsheets got me operating in virtue. The repetition of these activities, in turn, showed me the power of habit—new dispositions which got me off the plateau to where I am today. While the full and wondrous freedom of the third saintly stage still awaits, it already colors all of my daily struggles with purpose, motivation, and hope. Throughout the daily struggles and all the messiness, God has been truly *healing me*—in ways I never imagined possible. He longs to do the same for you.

Getting Past the Disappointing World of Problem-Solving

As our journey together has demonstrated, a virtue approach offers a therapy that surpasses all others. The plethora of popular self-help theories out there today includes some valuable gems, no doubt. Yet they tend to the Pelagian error that we can save ourselves. Still worse, they often promote understandings of the human person that are incomplete, unsatisfying, and even dangerous. Worst of all, by leaving God out, they frequently stay at the level of mere symptom-management, pain-alleviation, or problem-solving—never reaching the full purpose and prosperity that only grace makes possible.[1] The Church takes us so much further.

Transcending the shallow soundbites of today's drive-thru healing specials, our exploration into deeper healing has paved the way to the greatest happiness available. We have ventured deep into both Christ and who we are in Him. From God's dignifying image to the reality of our sinful condition, from the importance of humility to the role of baby steps in our redemption, from the power of prayer to the force of habit, we have definitively gotten beneath the surface. We have invited our Lord to search us and know us in our inmost regions, where we need divine mercy the most. In doing so, we have encountered healing that is thorough and lasting.

In contrast to the flat salvation-from-suffering that the secular self-help market is selling, we have come to understand healing as much more than the mere removal of negatives. More importantly, healing's elimination of disorder corresponds with the restoration of order and the presence of positives—such as healthy relationships, joy, hope, peace, fulfillment, vocational purpose, the meaning of redemptive suffering, and the freedom to be our best. Healing isn't just about overcoming whatever plagues us; it's about living joyfully.

While not an easy quick-fix, the holistic healing that we've been exploring is *real*. God's grace has made it so. The salvation that Christ offers surpasses the disappointing world of problem-solving. It unleashes vitality, and our redemption is more than worth the work. The Lord has plans to prosper us (Jer. 29:11), and *He* is worth the work. God does not break promises, nor does He disappoint. "For still the vision awaits its time; it hastens to the end—it will not lie. If it seem slow, wait for it; it will surely come, it will not delay" (Hab. 2:3). To paraphrase, "Hang in there, for God does not disappoint."

DISCUSSION

Ongoing Support from the Church: Conviction, Comfort, and Encouragement

For our concluding discussion, I'd like to highlight a few insights that stand out in a special way. Firstly, if you avail yourself of them, the writings of the Church will provide you with a source of tremendous support across your healing struggles. For instance, Pope Gregory the Great explains, "Certainly, in this world, the human spirit is like a boat foolishly fighting against the river's rush: one is never allowed to stay still, because unless one forges ahead, one will slide back downstream."[2] St. Bernard of Clairvaux says, "To not progress on the way of Life is to regress."[3] And Fr. James Keenan says, "To not follow is to retreat."[4] Such reminders supply us with the vital conviction that we must get back up and keep going whenever we fall.

At the same time, these treasured works remind us that the difficulties we experience mean we are doing something right. They help us realize that, if we were to feel comfortable, unchallenged, and remorseless about vice, *that's* when we'd be in trouble. Seen in the light of the Church, our difficulties are actually comforting!

Best of all, your ongoing study will assure you of God's forgiveness. As St. Bernard says,

> What are you afraid of ... that He will not pardon your sins? But with His own hands He has nailed them to the Cross ... where sin abounded, grace became superabundant ... what more can you wish?[5]

And as John Paul II explains in his apostolic exhortation, divine mercy "is a love more powerful than sin, stronger than death."[6]

Such anointed words are profoundly encouraging. They keep our difficulties in perspective, helping us to respond to them in grace instead of defeat. Scripture, papal encyclicals, the classic works of the saints—keep digging for treasure in these kingdom vaults, and you shall find conviction, comfort, and encouragement for the journey.

Echoes of Church Teaching

Second, it's worthy of note that our insights into virtue resonate throughout numerous areas. When I first discovered that the lifetime healing process is succinctly captured in the Church's presentation of virtue, the realization hit me as a surprise—and I wondered why I had never heard about it before. Actually, we all have.

In the writings of the mystics, these three stages mirror the "purgative, the illuminative, and the unitive."[7] In Teresa of Ávila's *Interior Castle*, they line up with our soul's advancement through the inner mansions.[8] In theology, they parallel the increase of God's image within us through the stages of "nature, grace, and glory."[9] In developmental psychology, they both overlap with and expand upon the categories of "childhood, adolescence, and adulthood."[10] In spiritual direction, they correspond with the three levels of "introductory moral motivation, intermediate catechesis, and advanced evocative-contemplation."[11] And they reflect the cycle of the Church in every generation, as described in the Book of the Apocalypse—through "purgation, illumination, and divine judgment."[12] To keep it simple, our threefold description of virtue describes the path of beatitude—which is absolutely central to life and, therefore, shows up everywhere.

Education versus Formation

Third, healing is a process of formation. Being a convert into Catholicism from an agnostic and then a Protestant past, I've experienced a special appreciation for the Catholic term *formation* ever since I first encountered it. I'd previously thought of this concept as our education. Yet the term "formation" is much richer than the term "education" — and far more accurate. It's not just our minds that are educated as we develop. Our whole complexity is being shaped, either lovingly or viciously, across time. We are being molded. Every interconnected part of our body-soul union is being formed.

Any secularist who would claim that he is "nonreligious" and therefore not in formation is wrong on both counts. He is in fact religious with regard to whatever his faith claims, worldview, and value system are — whether he is self-aware of his own presuppositions, or not. Moreover, his feelings, thinking, free will, spirit, and relationships are all being molded, or shaped, according to his daily decisions. The character of a secular relativist is being formed in moral relativism just as the character of a practicing Catholic is being formed in Christ. The Lord announced the happiness that awaits His people in the Beatitudes. He mentions elsewhere that those who reject God are on a different trajectory, are becoming something different, and have a different future awaiting them (Matt. 10:15).

APPLYING THE CONCEPTS ACROSS THE BOARD

The Case of the "Lazy" Student

One of my students took me up on virtue's three-stage curative in order to have God heal the vice of laziness. I opened our initial advising meeting by explaining to my student that he was not a problem to be fixed. I located and spoke to the surface various godly qualities I already saw in him. Life, love, freedom, and happiness — not the problem — set the stage for the student advisement process. When it came time to address the disorder and how exactly to bring healing, I encouraged him to tell me how he was feeling.

"I'm lazy," he repeated. "I just am. It's who I am, and I'm stuck like this. I guess it's in my DNA. It doesn't even make sense because I really do love learning. I know I'm smart, and it bothers me that my professors think otherwise. I can't blame them, though — most of my grades are D's. You'd think that since it bothers me, and since I enjoy education, that I'd do something about it! But I don't. Whenever a quiz, essay, or exam is coming up, I just don't want to study. Seems I'll always be this way."

I replied, "You *think* you don't want to study."

He corrected me, "No, I KNOW that I don't want to study."

I insisted, "No, you *think* that 'you know that you don't want to study.' Yet the real you *does* want to study. As you told me a moment ago, you love learning. The true you wants to study. So, the question is why you *think* you don't want to."

Beginning to smile, he replied, "OK, I'm following you — please, keep going."

"The answer is that what you think you want has been shaped by you, across time, through repeated actions that propelled your inclinations and character in the direction those actions were aiming you toward. Even though you love education, at moments in your past, you chose the tempting vice of laziness—which propelled you toward where you are now. Each time you chose it, the momentum increased. The vice internalized, and shaped your habits accordingly. In other words, laziness became second nature. You now think and feel as though you don't want to study—yet what you believe that you want has been shaped, by you, across time. I don't say this to blame you. On the contrary, I say this as an announcement of good news! Your tendencies can change."

"Keep going!" he said, now with hope in his voice.

I continued, "Thinking that you're stuck this way, it'll always be like this, and it's in your DNA is an outright lie. It's an error known as *determinism*. It falsely alleges that genetics and upbringing pre-determine us, and that we have no say in the matter. But the truth is that, while we're all certainly influenced by nature and nurture, we're never stuck this way. We have free will. I'd like to offer you a hands-on way forward. If you try it and it doesn't work, then you never have to see me again. If it works, then you'll be free. Either way, you have nothing to lose. Wanna hear it?"

"Lay it on me!"

After detailing the three-stage healing process, this student put it into action for himself, beginning with his own sticker chart. He didn't feel like studying at first, but he trusted the process. He studied for his next quiz, applied his smiley sticker to his chart, and aced the test. He did the same for each of his midterm exams. He also included reading assignments and essays as weekly sticker-earning duties on his spreadsheet. As the smiles accumulated, studying became routine. Eventually, he became a 4.0 student. The change made him contagiously joyful.

In our final advisement appointment together, I asked him what the keys were to his remarkable transformation. He began by admitting that he still had a long way to go, which indicated that humility girded him with truth (Eph. 6:14). That is, he was maintaining the elusive virtue, which bodes well for his continued victory. Then, he explained that the basis for his healing was twofold. The first key was the realization that what he believed he desired had been shaped, by him, across time, according to his daily living—and could be reshaped according to what was beneath the disorder, according to what he truly wanted and who he truly was. The second was his relationship with me—a caring mentor who saw the best in him, encouraged him, and took the time to help bring out his best.

He thus described grace, transmitted through relationship, which molded him across a virtue timeline. He described this pathway in detail, noting how (1) virtuous actions (2) internalized into habits that (3) came to mold his character—and he celebrated the blessings that the process reaped. In a word, he described *beatitude*.

The Choice between Two Roads

Each and every day we find two governing offices available to us: either (1) the happy reign of our trustworthy God, covenant faithfulness, freedom, and love (the kingship of God); or (2) empty promises that lead to relational fracture, heartache, and slavery (the kingship of this world). As we were born into the second, its misalignment, deception, and enticement *have to go*. It's the choice between life or death, between joy or heartbreak.

> He has placed before you fire and water: stretch out your hand for whichever you wish. Before a man are life and death, and whichever he chooses will be given to him. (Sir. 15:16–17)

As Peter said, "Lord, to whom shall we go? You have the words of eternal life" (John 6:68).

We are not problems to be fixed. We are the beloved reflections of our Creator's own perfect love, meant for abundant life. *You* are God's cherished! So, I pray that you will take the Great Physician up on His offer to heal you, both *from sin* and *for life*, and find out for yourself what it means to be more than a conqueror. If you try this threefold virtue approach, it will not be "found wanting."[13] It will be found flourishing—and you'll wonder why you didn't try it sooner.

NOTES

Introduction

1. Ricoeur, Paul, *Time and Narrative, Volume 1*, trans. Kathleen McLaughlin and David Pellauer. (Chicago: University of Chicago Press, 1984), p. 72.

Chapter 1

1. Vost, Kevin, *The Seven Deadly Sins: A Thomistic Guide to Vanquishing Vice and Sin*, (Manchester: Sophia Institute Press, 2015).
2. Augustine, *Confessions*, trans. Rex Warner. (New York: Penguin Books, 1963), Book 6, Chapter VIII.
3. Aristotle, *Nicomachean Ethics*, 2nd edition, trans. Terence Irwin. (Indianapolis: Hackett Publishing Company), 1119b. (Original work composed around 340 BC.)
4. Aquinas, Thomas, *Prayer before Study*. Published in the Raccolta #764, Pius XI *Studiorum Ducem*, 29 June, 1923. (Original work composed around the mid-13th century.)
5. Aristotle, *Ethics*, 1119b.

Chapter 2

1. *Beachbody*. (Beverly Hills: Product Partners, LLC, 2007).
2. *A Catholic Christian Meta-Model of the Person*, ed. Paul C. Vitz, William J. Nordling, and Craig Steven Titus (Sterling: Divine Mercy University Press, 2020), pp. xi–xiii.

3. Aquinas, Thomas, *Summa Theologica* I q. 93, art. 4, trans. English Dominican Province. (Westminster, MD: Christian Classics, 1948). (Original work composed 1265–1273.)

4. Pinckaers, Servais, *The Sources of Christian Ethics*, trans. Sr. Mary Thomas Noble (Washington, DC: The Catholic University of America Press, 1995).

5. Pinckaers, Servais, "Morality and the Movement of the Holy Spirit: Aquinas's Doctrine of 'Instinctus,'" *The Pinckaers Reader: Renewing Thomistic Moral Theology*, trans. J. Berkman and Craig Steven Titus (Washington, DC: The Catholic University of America Press), p. 394.

6. Grossman, Miriam. *Unprotected: A Campus Psychiatrist Reveals How Political Correctness in Her Profession Endangers Every Student.* (New York: Sentinel Trade, 2007).

7. Ibid.

8. Doidge, N. *The Brain that Changes Itself: Stories of Personal Triumph from the Frontiers of Brain Science*, (New York: Penguin, 2007), p. 427. See also Bridges, A. J. *Pornography's Effects on Interpersonal Relationships*, (Princeton, NJ: Witherspoon Institute, 2010) and Reeder, H. *It Doesn't Hurt to Look, Does It? The Real Effect of Pornography on Relationships*, (May 7, 2014).

9. Vitz, Paul C. "Addressing Moderate Interpersonal Hatred before Addressing Forgiveness in Psychotherapy and Counseling: A Proposed Model," *Journal of Religion and Health* 57, no. 2 (2018), pp. 725–737.

10. Ashley, B. M. *Healing for Freedom: A Christian Perspective on Personhood and Psychotherapy*, (Arlington, VA: The Institute for the Psychological Sciences Press, 2013), pp. 322–331.

Chapter 3

1. Vitz, Paul C. "Modern Personality Theories: A Critical Understanding of Personality from a Catholic Christian Perspective," *A Catholic Christian Meta-Model of the Person*, ed. Paul C. Vitz, William J. Nordling, and Craig Steven Titus (Sterling: Divine Mercy University Press, 2020), pp. 64–65.

2. For Tolkien's understanding of the relationship between his fantasy narratives and Catholic doctrine, see Tolkien, J. R. R. "On Fairy-Stories," *The Tolkien Reader: Stories, Poems, and Commentary by the Author of "The Hobbit" and "The Lord of the Rings"*, (New York: Ballantine Books, 1966), pp. 3–84.

3. Vitz, "Modern Personality Theories," pp. 63–64. See also Sweeney, G., C. S. Titus, and W. Nordling, "Training Psychologists and Christian Anthropology," *Edification* 3 no.1, (2009), pp. 51–56.

4. Nordling, William J., Paul C. Vitz, and Craig Steven Titus. "Introduction to a Catholic Christian Meta-Model of the Person for Mental Health Practice," *A Catholic Christian Meta-Model of the Person*, ed. Paul C. Vitz, William J. Nordling, and Craig Steven Titus. (Sterling: Divine Mercy University Press, 2020), pp. 3–19.

5. For instance, the "positive psychology" movement advanced by Dr. Martin Seligman has made tremendous strides toward achieving a more holistic view in psychological scholarship, and therefore, toward more thorough approaches to healing. Such contributions ought to be respected, appreciated, and welcomed with open arms. At the same time, it's important to remember the limitations of any clinical research that leaves God out of the analyses.

6. John Paul II, "Preface," *Fides et Ratio*, (Vatican, VA: Libreria Editrice Vaticana, 1998). See also paragraph n. 22 of the same, which

describes how human reasoning can "wake up" faith. By "discoursing on the data provided by the senses," human reasoning can actually take us to the "cause which lies at the origin of all perceptible reality." In other words—and excitingly—human reason can lead a seeking person to the necessary reality of the transcendent.

7. Duffy, R., E. Bott, B. Allan, C. Torrey, and B. Dik, "Perceiving a Calling, Living a Calling, and Job Satisfaction: Testing a Moderated, Multiple Mediator Model," *Journal of Counseling Psychology* 59 no. 1 (2012), pp. 50–59.

8. Benedict XVI. *Caritas in Veritate*, (Vatican, VA: Libreria Editrice Vaticana, 2009), n. 31.

9. John Paul II. *Reconciliatio et Paenitentia*, (Vatican: Libreria Editrice Vaticana, 1984), n. 22.

10. Nordling, Vitz, and Titus. "Introduction to a Catholic Christian Meta-Model," p. 4.

11. Pinckaers, Servais. *Sources of Christian Ethics*, (Washington, DC: The Catholic University of America Press, 1995), p. 375. See also Ashley, *Healing for Freedom*, p. 212.

12. Keenan, James. *Moral Wisdom: Lessons and Texts from the Catholic Tradition*, (Lanham, MD: The Rowman & Littlefield Publishing Group, 2004), pp. 146–152.

Chapter 4

1. Titus, Craig Steven, Paul C. Vitz, and William J. Nordling. "Created in the Image of God," *A Catholic Christian Meta-Model of the Person*, ed. Paul C. Vitz, William J. Nordling, and Craig Steven Titus. (Sterling: Divine Mercy University Press, 2020), pp. 449–472.

2. Benedict XVI. Address of his Holiness Benedict XVI on the *Occasion of Christmas Greetings to the Roman Curia*, (Clementine Hall, Thursday, December 22, 2011), n. 5.

3. Titus, Vitz, and Nordling, "Created in the Image of God," p. 453.

4. International Theological Commission, *Communion and Stewardship: Human Persons Created in the Image of God,* (Vatican, VA: Libreria Editrice Vaticana, 2002), n. 10.

5. John Paul II. *Redemptor Hominis,* (Vatican, VA: Libreria Editrice Vaticana, 1979), n. 10.

6. Quoted in Aquilina, Mike, *The Way of the Fathers: Praying with the Early Christians,* (Huntington: Our Sunday Visitor, 2000), p. 27.

Chapter 5

1. This idea that "all truth is God's truth" is common throughout Christian history. As Clement of Alexandria states, "Who, then, is the King of all? God, who is the measure of the truth of all existence." In "Chapter VI," *Exhortation to the Heathen,* (Pickerington: Beloved Publishing, 2016). (Original work composed 195 AD.) Augustine says, "Nay, but let every good and true Christian understand that wherever truth may be found, it belongs to his Master" in *On Christian Doctrine,* trans. J. F. Shaw. (Mineola: Dover Publications, 2009) (II.18). (Original work composed around 400 AD.) Following Clement and Augustine, Aquinas and Calvin each develop the idea in more detail. For instance, in his commentary on Titus 1:12, Calvin says, "All truth is from God; and consequently, if wicked men have said anything that is true and just, we ought not to reject it; for it has come from God." These are but a few of the plentiful examples.

2. Benedict XVI. *Deus Caritas Est,* (Vatican, VA: Libreria Editrice Vaticana, 2005), n. 7.

3. Augustine. *Letter 118.* Quoted in Aquilina, *Way of the Fathers*, p. 129. (Original work composed 410 AD.)

4. Mother Teresa. *In the Heart of the World: Thoughts, Stories, and Prayers,* (Novato: New World Library, 1997).

Chapter 6

1. Scholtz, Tom. "More than a Feeling," *Boston*, (Foxglove: Epic Records, 1976).

2. Merton, Thomas. See Thurston, Bonnie, *"I Spoke Most of Prayer": Thomas Merton on the West Coast,* (September 11– October 15, 1968), p. 16. Retrieved from http://merton.org/ ITMS/Seasonal/35/35-3Thurston.pdf.

3. Murphy, Ian. *Dying to Live: From Agnostic to Baptist to Catholic,* (San Francisco: Ignatius Press, 2020), pp. 14–15.

4. Fr. James Dominic Brent, interviewed by Sr. Hope, SV. *Imprint*, (Suffern, NY: Sisters of Life, Winter 2020), pp. 3–5.

Chapter 7

1. Murphy, *Dying to Live*, 209.

2. Titus, Craig Steven, Paul C. Vitz, and William J. Nordling, "Personal Wholeness," *A Catholic Christian Meta-Model of the Person,* ed. Paul C. Vitz, William J. Nordling, and Craig Steven Titus, (Sterling: Divine Mercy University Press, 2020), pp. 145–168.

3. Ibid., 147.

4. Ashley, *Healing for Freedom*, 156–166.

5. Aquinas, I. q. 75, arts. 3–51.

6. Pinckaers, Servais. "Conscience and Christian Tradition," *The Pinckaers Reader: Renewing Thomistic Moral Theology*, trans. J. Berkman and Craig Steven Titus, (Washington, DC: The Catholic University of America Press), pp. 321–341.

7. Pascal, Blaise. *Pensées*, (New York: E. P. Dutton, n. d), para. 347. (Original work composed around the mid-17th century.)
8. John Paul II. "Preface," *Fides et Ratio*. See also nn. 15, 67.
9. Ibid., nn. 46, 53.
10. Augustine. "Book 1, Chapter 1," *Confessions*, trans. F. J. Sheed, ed. Michael P. Foley, (Indianapolis: Hackett Publishing Company, 2006). (Original work composed around 400 AD.)
11. Titus, Craig Steven and P. Scrofani. "The Art of Love: A Roman Catholic Psychology of Love," *Journal of Psychology and Christianity* 31, no. 2 (2012), pp. 118–129.
12. Gross, Christopher, Craig Steven Titus, Paul C. Vitz, and William J. Nordling. "Emotional," *A Catholic Christian Meta-Model of the Person*, ed. Paul C. Vitz, William J. Nordling, and Craig Steven Titus, (Sterling: Divine Mercy University Press, 2020), pp. 355–370.
13. Titus, Vitz, and Nordling, "Personal Wholeness," pp. 152–153.
14. Ibid.
15. Ibid., p. 151.

Chapter 8

1. Nordling, Vitz, and Titus, "Introduction to a Catholic Christian Meta-Model," p. 4.
2. Aquinas, Thomas. *Summa Theologica*, I–II, q. 85, arts. 1–2. See also International Theological Commission (ITC), 2002. *Communion and Stewardship: Human Persons Created in the Image of God* (n. 48).
3. Augustine, *Confessions* (Sheed translation), Book 8, Chapter VII.
4. Catholic Church. "The Eucharist — Source and Summit of Ecclesial Life," *Catechism of the Catholic Church*, (Vatican City: Libreria Editrice Vaticana, 1994), n. 1330.

Chapter 9

1. McInerny, D. "Poised Strength," *Philosophical Virtues and Psychological Strengths*, ed. R. Cessario, Craig Steven Titus, and Paul C. Vitz, (Manchester: Sophia Institute Press, 2013), pp. 201–202.
2. Gondreau, P. "Balanced Emotions," *Philosophical Virtues and Psychological strengths*, ed. R. Cessario, Craig Steven Titus, and Paul C. Vitz, (Manchester: Sophia Institute Press, 2013), pp. 145–146.
3. Gross, Titus, and Vitz, "Emotional," pp. 355–370.
4. Levering, Matthew. *Biblical Natural Law: A Theocentric and Teleological Approach*, (New York, NY: Oxford University Press, 2008), p. 221.

Chapter 10

1. Retrieved from iliketoquote.com.
2. John Paul II. *Marriage in the Integral Vision of Man*, General Audience: April 2, 1980.

Chapter 11

1. Tyler, J. E. A. *The Tolkien Companion*, ed. S. A. Tyler, illus. Kevin Reilly, (New York, NY: St. Martin's Press, 1976), p. 25.
2. Pinckaers, *Sources*, 1–44, pp. 354–468.
3. Augustine. *Of the Morals of the Catholic Church*, trans. Richard Stothert. (Savage: Lighthouse Christian Publishing, 2017), ch. 15, n. 25. (Original work composed 388 AD.)
4. Harris III, James, and Terry Lewis. "Human," *Human League*, (Hollywood: A&M Records, 1986).
5. Nordling, Vitz, and Titus, "Introduction to a Catholic Christian Meta-Model," p. 5.
6. Aquinas, I. q. 65, arts. 1.

7. Aristotle, *Ethics*, 1104a.
8. Aquinas, I. q. 64, arts. 1.

Chapter 12

1. Dunnington explains a useful distinction between "free will," which refers to someone's volitional ability to choose in accord with wisdom, versus "willpower," which refers to the amount of moral strength that a person currently possesses for resisting temptation and doing the good. A certain virtuous stride may in fact lay beyond the limits of a person's willpower. Yet the person still has the free will to take a virtuous baby step in the right direction. The two notions are closely related in that the proper exercise of a person's *free will* strengthens the person's *willpower* over time. No matter how weak or strong a person is at any given point in their development, living virtuously is always a matter of using one's free will to choose the next virtuous baby step forward in the present moment. See Dunnington, K. "Addiction and Sin: Testing an Ancient Doctrine," *Addiction and Virtue: Beyond the Models of Disease and Choice*, (Downers Grove, IL: InterVarsity Press Academic, 2010), pp. 125–140.
2. I am grateful to Justin Fatica for the phrase "Look up, get back up, and don't give up."
3. Pieper, J. *Leisure: The Basis of Culture*, (San Francisco: Ignatius Press, 2009), pp. 29–30.
4. Berkman, John. "Introduction," *The Pinckaers Reader: Renewing Thomistic Moral Theology*, ed. John Berkman and Craig Steven Titus. (Washington, D. C.: The Catholic University of America Press, 2005), pp. xi–xxiii.
5. Aquinas, I. q. 55, arts. 2–4.
6. Ibid., q. 55, aa. 1–2. See also q. 49, a. 3.

Chapter 13

1. Aquinas, Thomas. Quoted by the Christian History Institute, *Article #29*. Retrieved from https://christianhistoryinstitute. org/incontext/article/aquinas.

2. Aquinas, I. q. 55, arts. 2; q. 55 arts. 1; q. 51, arts. 2; q. 52, arts. 3. Italics added for emphasis. See also q. 49, arts. 3.

3. Doidge, *The Brain that Changes Itself*, p. 427. See also Shatz, C. J. "The Developing Brain," *Scientific American*, (1992), pp. 60–67. Cited by Titus, C. S., Nordling, W., and Vitz, P. *Fulfilled in Virtue*, (Washington, DC: Institute for the Psychological Sciences, 2015), p. 6.

4. Titus, Nordling, & Vitz, *Fulfilled in Virtue*, p. 6.

5. Gondreau, "Balanced Emotions," pp. 145–146.

6. Teresa of Ávila. *The Life of Teresa of Jesus: The Autobiography of Teresa of Ávila*, ed. E. Allison Peers, (New York: Image Books by special arrangement with Sheed & Ward, 1960), p. 6. (Original work composed beginning in June, 1562.)

7. Meshorer, Sean. *The Bliss Experiment: 28 Days to Personal Transformation*, (New York: Atria Paperback, 2012), p. 77. Meshorer attributes the claim that "habits develop in as few as fifty repetitions" to a habit-formation study published in the journal *Neuroscience*.

8. Lally, Phillippa, Cornelia H. M. Van Jaarsveld, Henry W. W. Potts, and Jane Wardle. "How are Habits Formed: Modeling Habit Formation in the Real World," *European Journal of Social Psychology* 40, (2010), pp. 998–1009. (Originally published July 16th, 2009.)

9. Ibid.

10. Chesterton, G. K. *What's Wrong with the World?* (NY: Cassell and Company, Ltd., 1910), p. 48.

Chapter 14

1. Brent, *Imprint*, p. 4.
2. Aquinas, I. q. 55, arts.3. Italics added for emphasis.
3. Benedict XVI. *Spes Salvi*, (Vatican, VA: Libreria Editrice Vaticana, 2007), n. 33. Benedict is quoting St. Augustine's *Homily on the First Letter of John*.
4. John Paul II, *Veritatis Splendor*, Vatican, VA: Libreria Editrice Vaticana, 1993), n. 15.
5. Murphy, *Dying to Live*, 47.

Chapter 15

1. Tolkien, J. R. R. *The Hobbit*, (Boston: Houghton Mifflin Company, 1937), pp. 159–160.
2. Ashley, B. M. *Healing for Freedom: A Christian Perspective on Personhood and Psychotherapy*, (Arlington, VA: The Institute for the Psychological Sciences Press, 2013), pp. 317–325.
3. Ibid., pp. 341–342.
4. Augustine, *Confessions* (Sheed translation), Book 8, Chap. XI.
5. Selk, Jason. "Habit Formation: The 21-Day Myth," *Forbes*, (2013). Retrieved from https://www.forbes.com/sites/jasonselk/2013/04/15/habit-formation-the-21-day-myth/?sh=7f9e95e1debc.
6. Ibid.
7. Augustine, *Confessions* (Sheed translation), Book 8, Chap. XI.
8. Gregory XVI. *Summo Iugiter Studio*, (Papal Encyclicals Online, 2020), n. 6. Retrieved from https://www.papalencyclicals.net/greg16/g16summo.htm. (Encyclical originally promulgated in 1832.)

Chapter 16

1. Aquinas, I. q. 65, arts. 1.

2. St. Mother Teresa, *In the Heart of the World*.

3. Aquilina, Mike. *Love in the Little Things: Tales of Family Life*, (Cincinnati, OH: Servant, an imprint of Franciscan Media, 2007).

4. Aquinas, I. q. 162, arts. 1.

5. Martin, Ralph. *The Fulfillment of All Desire: A Guidebook for the Journey to God Based on the Wisdom of the Saints*, (Steubenville, OH: Emmaus Road Publishing, 2006), p. 145.

Chapter 17

1. Sweeney, Titus, & Nordling, "Training Psychologists," *Edification*, pp. 51–56.

2. Gregory the Great. *Reg. Past.*, p. III, c. 34. Quoted by Keenan, *Moral Wisdom*, p. 29.

3. Bernard of Clairvaux. *Serm. II*, n. 3. Quoted by Keenan, *Moral Wisdom*, p. 29.

4. Keenan, *Moral Wisdom*, p. 29.

5. Bernard of Clairvaux, *On the Song of Songs*, vol. II, sermon 38, n. 2, p. 188. Cited by Martin, *Fulfillment of All Desire*, pp. 28–29.

6. John Paul II. *Reconciliatio et Paenitentia*, n. 22.

7. John of the Cross. *Dark Night of the Soul*, trans. E. Allison Peers, (Mineola, NY: Dover Publications, Inc., 2003). (Original work composed 1577–1579.)

8. Teresa of Ávila. *The Interior Castle*, trans. Mirabai Starr, (New York: Riverhead Books, 2003). (Original work composed 1577.)

9. Aquinas, I. q. 93, arts. 4. See also ITC, 2002, n. 16.

10. Titus, C. S. *A Virtue Approach to Psychology and the Helping Professions*, (Washington, DC: Institute for the Psychological Sciences, 2015), p. 7.

11. Coombs, Marie Theresa and Francis Kelly Nemeck. *The Spiritual Journey: Critical Thresholds and Stages of Adult Spiritual Genesis*, (Collegeville, MN: The Liturgical Press, 1990).

12. Schüssler Fiorenza, Elisabeth. *The Book of Revelation: Justice and Judgment*, 2nd ed, (Minneapolis, MN: Fortress Press, 1998).

13. Chesterton, *What's Wrong with the World*, p. 48.

Sophia Institute

SOPHIA INSTITUTE IS a nonprofit institution that seeks to nurture the spiritual, moral, and cultural life of souls and to spread the gospel of Christ in conformity with the authentic teachings of the Roman Catholic Church.

Sophia Institute Press fulfills this mission by offering translations, reprints, and new publications that afford readers a rich source of the enduring wisdom of mankind.

Sophia Institute also operates the popular online resource CatholicExchange.com. *Catholic Exchange* provides world news from a Catholic perspective as well as daily devotionals and articles that will help readers to grow in holiness and live a life consistent with the teachings of the Church.

In 2013, Sophia Institute launched Sophia Institute for Teachers to renew and rebuild Catholic culture through service to Catholic education. With the goal of nurturing the spiritual, moral, and cultural life of souls, and an abiding respect for the role and work of teachers, we strive to provide materials and programs that are at once enlightening to the mind and ennobling to the heart; faithful and complete, as well as useful and practical.

Sophia Institute gratefully recognizes the Solidarity Association for preserving and encouraging the growth of our apostolate over the course of many years. Without their generous and timely support, this book would not be in your hands.

www.SophiaInstitute.com
www.CatholicExchange.com
www.SophiaInstituteforTeachers.org

Sophia Institute Press is a registered trademark of Sophia Institute.
Sophia Institute is a tax-exempt institution as defined by the
Internal Revenue Code, Section 501(c)(3). Tax ID 22-2548708.